Stasi State or Socialist Paradise?
The German Democratic Republic
and what became of it

by Bruni de la Motte and John Green

Stasi State or Socialist Paradise? The German Democratic Republic and what became of it

by Bruni de la Motte & John Green

First published in Britain in 2015
Copyright © Bruni de la Motte and John Green

Designed by Michal Boncza

Printed by Russell Press

ACIP catalogue record for this book is available from the British Library
ISBN 978-0-9558228-6-5

Artery Publications, 11 Dorset Road, London W5 4HU

CONTENTS

'The truth, is so often the reverse of what has been told us by our culture that we cannot turn our heads far enough around to see it.'

Howard Zinn (1970)

'I am convinced there is only one way to eliminate these grave evils [of capitalist society] namely through the establishment of a socialist economy, accompanied by an educational system which would be oriented toward social goals. In such an economy, the means of production are owned by society itself and are utilised in a planned fashion. A planned economy, which adjusts production to the needs of the community, would distribute the work to be done among all those able to work and would guarantee a livelihood to every man, woman, and child. The education of the individual, in addition to promoting his own innate abilities, would attempt to develop in him a sense of responsibility for his fellow men in place of the glorification of power and success in our present society.'

Albert Einstein (1949)

FOREWORD

History is famously written by the victors. Nowhere is that more obvious than in the former communist states of central and eastern Europe. Their successor governments have systematically sought to demonise or even punish any attempt to recognise the social and economic achievements of east European-style socialism, alongside its constantly rehearsed failures and injustices.

The more their citizens balk at such a one-sided account of their own lived experiences, the more any honest or remotely sympathetic discussion of the experience of post-war European communism is met with official denunciation and legal bans, from Hungary to Ukraine.

In the case of the former German Democratic Republic, the drive to brand it an illegitimate 'state of injustice' and deny the existence of any redeeming features has become a test of loyalty in today's Federal Republic. The great merit of Bruni de la Motte and John Green's book is that, far from whitewashing the East German experience, it offers a sober and balanced assessment - neither exaggerating its successes nor downplaying its failings.

The GDR was home to the Stasi, shortages and the Berlin wall. But it was also a country of full employment, social and women's equality well ahead of its time, cheap housing, transport and culture, one of the best childcare systems in the world, and greater freedom in the workplace than most employees enjoy in today's Germany.

Along with the humiliation of West Germany's takeover, that's why *Der Spiegel* found in 2009 that 57 per cent of eastern Germans believed the GDR had "more good sides

1

than bad sides", and even younger people rejected the idea that the state had been a dictatorship. Similar public disenchantment with the post-1989 experience can be found in polling results across eastern Europe and the former Soviet Union.

For Germans, of course, the destruction of the wall didn't only signal the end of authoritarian rule and travel restrictions in the east, competitive elections and better consumer goods, as elsewhere in the former eastern bloc. It also meant an end to the militarised division of families, their capital city and an entire nation. So they had more reason to celebrate than most.

But the question in 1989 wasn't whether the old system had to change - it was how it would change. The political force that had turned the Soviet Union into a superpower, industrialised half of Europe and sent the first human being into space had exhausted itself. There were, however, alternative routes out of its crisis.

What the protesters in first Gdansk and then Leipzig were mostly demanding was not capitalism, but a different kind of socialism. Even given a restoration of capitalism, there were softer landings that could have been negotiated between the main Cold War powers.

Instead, 1989 unleashed across the region and then the former Soviet Union free-market shock therapy, commercial robbery dressed up as privatisation, vast increases in inequality, and poverty and joblessness for tens of millions. Reunification in Germany meant annexation, the takeover and closure of most of its industry, a political purge of more than a million teachers and other white-collar workers, a loss of women's rights, closure of free nurseries and mass unemployment – still almost double western Germany's rate after a quarter of a century.

And east Germany has done far better than the rest. Elsewhere in eastern Europe, the crisis created under western tutelage was comparable to the Great Depression in the US, and national income took more than a decade to recover. In Russia itself, post-communist catastroika produced the greatest peacetime economic collapse in modern history.

The western failure to recognise the shocking price paid by many east Europeans for a highly qualified freedom – the *Economist* contemptuously dismissed them as "the old, the timid, the dim" – is only exceeded by the refusal to acknowledge that the communist system had benefits as well as obvious costs.

This two-sided nature of 1989 is also reflected in its global and ideological impact. It kicked off the process that led to the end of the Cold War. But by removing the world's only other superpower from the global stage, it also destroyed the constraints on US global power and paved the way for wars from the Gulf and Yugoslavia to Iraq and Afghanistan.

At the same time, by destroying its main ideological competitor, 1989 opened the door to a deregulated model of capitalism that has wreaked social and economic havoc across the world. That, in turn, led to the economic crash of 2008, which discredited - but has far from sunk - that neoliberal model. But it also created the conditions for the wave of progressive change in Latin America that has challenged the post-89 social order and raised the possibility of a new form of socialism for the 21st century.

It's often said that the collapse of European communism and the Soviet Union has destroyed the only systemic alternative to capitalism. But the pressure for a social alternative has always come from capitalism itself and its failures, which are once again increasingly obvious to people throughout the world.

The system that collapsed a generation ago is history. But, as new movements and models emerge to challenge a global order beset by ecological and economic crisis, it's crucial to learn the lessons of both its successes and failures.

By laying out the experience of 40 years of the GDR, which they describe as having been 'one of the most egalitarian societies in Europe', Bruni de la Motte and John Green have performed a valuable service for the future.

Seumas Milne

INTRODUCTION

The year 2015 marks the 70th anniversary of perhaps the most decisive event of the 20th century: the defeat of fascism and the end of the Second World War. The allied victory over fascism laid the basis for the restructuring of our post war world and brought into being two German states – the Federal Republic of Germany (FRG) and the German Democratic Republic (GDR). The GDR existed for 40 years, until 1990, when a majority of its citizens voted for unification with the Federal Republic. The history and experience of the GDR has been much commented on, but almost exclusively from the perspective of the 'victors'. This casts the GDR as a historical anomaly: a totalitarian and oppressive system with few if any redeeming facets.

One of the most widely-read books on the GDR that has helped cement that mainstream narrative is Anna Funder's *Stasiland*. Tens of thousands of copies have been printed and it has been translated into many languages. It has become, for many, the definitive portrait of the GDR. There is neither the space here nor the inclination to detail the numerous basic errors and profound misinformation her book contains. It reflects the pre-conceived mindset of an outsider who had only visited the GDR, fleetingly, once and who grasped with both hands the opportunity of providing the Stasi horror story that Western publishers were more than happy to print.

It is a truism that if you have never actually lived in a country any attempt at a balanced assessment of life in it is going to be based on second-hand information and hearsay. To judge any country simply on Western media reports, selective statistics or the views of dissidents is to accept a one-dimensional picture, and that is what most commentators have done with the communist-run countries.

Most mainstream western observers characterise the GDR experience as just another dark period in German and European history – a country ruled oppressively by a totalitarian regime. It could, though, be more accurately described as an idealistic attempt to build a democratic and socialist state on the embers of German fascism which, for a variety of reasons, fell far short of that ideal.

The process of demonisation and the lurid descriptions of life in the GDR as conveyed in the mainstream media have been made largely by outsiders and from a Western perspective, in the main by West Germans. While there have been many GDR eyewitness accounts, only those that conform to that West German establishment narrative have been given publicity and credence.

Of course, as in any society, there were in the GDR those who disliked the system and suffered, as well as those who were relatively indifferent and those who actively or passively supported it. However, it is only those who were opponents and dissidents who have been given the oxygen of publicity. The state security apparatus, known as the Stasi, has been depicted as defining the whole socialist system.

Understandably, many former GDR citizens feel this narrative is not only extremely biased but that its aim is to diminish, if not erase, the meaning of their own lives and careers as GDR citizens. This book is an attempt to present a more differentiated picture, one that challenges the establishment's hegemonic narrative on the basis of readily available facts and from first hand experience.

The GDR was a much more complex historical phenomenon and society than is generally portrayed in the mainstream literature and media. Its achievements were in many ways quite phenomenal, particularly given the appallingly low starting point in 1945 amid the devastation left by Hitler fascism and the war as well as continuous post-war attempts to stifle it through isolation, trade embargoes and even sabotage. It is an attempt to portray life in the GDR and to demonstrate that the 'Stasi Hell' Funder and others describe was not the reality that the majority shared and that, despite all the problems, its citizens did make some significant advances, even if these did not amount to a workers' paradise.

While the East European communist-led countries imploded after 1989, in the wake of Gorbachev's reforms, market capitalism in the West was enjoying a buoyant new lease of life. All Western leaders declared that we had to embrace global 'free-market' capitalism as there was no alternative - the 'end of history' was proclaimed. Since then, world capitalism has entered one of its periodic deep crises. As this affected ever more people and the well-being of entire societies, questions began to be asked more forcibly about possible alternatives to the system. Could socialism perhaps be the answer after all, despite the fact that the Eastern European versions failed?

It is 25 years since the GDR disappeared from history, but the perceived need on the part of western leaders to continue to vilify and denigrate that experience is as strong as ever. The attempt to build socialism in one part of Germany is being demonised and the whole experience portrayed as parallel to the Nazi period, as the 'second of the two dictatorships'. Why is this? Is there, perhaps, a hidden agenda to negate the very idea of imagining a different, socialist form of society?

Our aim in this book is to present a more detailed picture of how GDR society actually functioned in terms of the daily life of its people, what its basic values and principles were and what their impact was on the social interrelationships of the people who lived there. Our first booklet about the GDR, *Stasi Hell or Workers' Paradise?* was published six years before this one and found a wide interest. Rather than continue to reprint that book, we decided it would make more sense to rework, expand its scope and to include what actually happened on the territory of the former GDR since unification and the impact it has had on the people who live there.

Seen through the eyes of those who today live in one of the more advanced and wealthy capitalist democracies, the GDR would have fallen short on a whole number of democratic rights, but where its strengths lay was in the field of economic democracy. As Tony Benn so often quite rightly emphasised: democracy is about much more than voting for a choice of parties every four years or so. The whole question of economic democracy – rights in the workplace, egalitarian fiscal and taxation measures, gender equality and empowerment of communities – is rarely discussed in western societies or even seen as an integral aspect of any nation which calls itself democratic.

While the GDR was an authoritarian state, there was, on the part of many in the leadership and many thousands of ordinary citizens, the genuine aim of trying to build a socialist, more equitable, just and peaceable society in the wake of a devastating war. It is quite possible that the denigration of the GDR by the West German establishment has more to do with atoning for what it failed to do after the war, i.e. bring to justice all those who played a prominent role in the Nazi regime and to re-educate a new generation about the evils of Nazism.

Irrespective of how history finally judges the GDR, tens of thousands of GDR citizens at all levels of society genuinely believed in, and worked most of their lives in an attempt to build a new, democratic society on the ruins of Hitler's 'eternal Reich'. They had to battle not only enemies without, but the dogmatists, careerists, opportunists and hangers-on in their own society. To deny this truth and this aspect of life in the GDR is to distort history unforgivably.

'Ostalgie' – the term used by West Germans to describe any positive remarks about the GDR made by ex-GDR citizens – is not simply a looking back at the past through rose-tinted spectacles. The GDR did, despite all the warts, represent the germ of a better form of society to that existing in most capitalist countries. It was based on solidarity, people were united by a common purpose, the collective good came before individual egoism and personal wealth, consumerism played a minor role in people's lives. Those values still informed the consciousness of many former GDR citizens, even several years after unification and are seen as positive in contrast to the elbow society values of consumer capitalism. They are also values we need to recover if we wish to build healthier societies.

This book challenges the mainstream narrative and argues for a more differentiated historical analysis, one that helps the reader better understand and comprehend how the GDR arose and what it actually represented and achieved. But, above all, the authors hope the facts and evidence provided here will also help those with an interest in building a more just and socialist society in the future to gain insights from the GDR experience, from both its positive and negative sides.

A DIFFICULT BIRTH –
HOW THE GDR CAME ABOUT

In the immediate aftermath of the war large sections of the German population yearned for real change: demoralised and traumatised by the war, many realised that the Nazis, with the collaboration of the big financiers and industrialists, had perpetrated a cruel historical experiment on the nation.

As in Britain, the majority of the population was sick of war and the injustices of the past and was demanding a more just and equitable society. In all four occupied sectors of Germany, there was widespread demand for the expropriation of the big banks, utilities and Nazi-supporting industrialists, a genuine de-nazification and democratic reform – and these demands were being made not only by left-wing parties, but across the political spectrum.

In 1946, referendums were held in Saxony, in the Soviet zone, as well as in Hesse, in the US zone of occupation. In Saxony, voters were asked to approve or reject a proposal to expropriate large landowners and those big industrialists who had been active Nazi supporters and war criminals. It was proposed that these large industries be taken into public ownership. Over 77 per cent of votes cast were in favour of these proposals.

Two referendums were held in Hesse, one on a new constitution – the most progressive proposal to be voted on in the US zone – in which voters were asked whether they supported Article 41 on the nationalisation of essential industries and banks. Over 62 per cent voted in favour. The US occupying forces then organised a further referendum on Article 41 (clearly in the hope that it would be defeated), but 72 per cent then voted in favour. Article 41 stated that, 'the mining industry (coal, ore and potash), iron and steel industry, energy companies and railways should be placed under public control; large banks and insurance companies should be regulated or administered by the state.'

In contrast to what happened in the Soviet zone, the western occupying forces chose to ignore these demands carried by overwhelming majorities. Similar referendums were also held in Berlin and North Rhine-Westphalia, in the British zone, both of which also gave majorities for expropriation. However, with the immediate onset of the Cold War and the West's fear of the spread of socialist thinking, these democratic decisions were vetoed by the western occupying powers.[1]

Within weeks of the end of the war, the Soviet occupation forces encouraged the re-establishment of trade unions, cultural organisations and political parties. Already by July 1945, a Kulturbund (Cultural League for the Democratic renewal of Germany) was set up in the Soviet sector to assist with the re-opening of theatres, music venues and cinemas and to promote Germany's democratic cultural legacy as an antidote to Hitler's fascist de-culturalisation and xenophobia. It took another three months before the formation of political parties and trade unions were permitted in the US sector, which also hindered the setting up of cultural organisations, fearing that they would rapidly become dominated by communists and leftist forces.

In the Soviet zone, which later became the GDR, there was a determined effort to eliminate Nazi ideology and to remove those who were either war criminals or top Nazi activists from all positions of power as stipulated in the Potsdam Agreement reached between the allies in 1945. Many of the guilty who had been implicated or had taken an active part in committing atrocities inflicted on Russia and Eastern Europe by the Nazis fled to the West before they could be brought to justice. There they were able to enjoy a comfortable and undisturbed life. Although the GDR made a substantial and largely successful effort to eradicate Nazi influence on its territory, some historians today are attempting to question its anti-fascist credentials and now prefer to characterise the GDR itself as a successor to the Nazis, in terms of its ideology, its party and state structures.

The GDR was created, almost as a historical accident, in October 1949, out of the former Soviet zone of occupation in Germany. It came about as a response to the introduction of a separate currency in the Western sectors in the summer of 1949, followed by the go-it-alone creation of the Federal Republic in September of that same year. It is another one of those 'forgotten' historical facts that it was the Western allies' surprise introduction of a new currency in the three zones occupied by the Western allies and West Berlin which led the Soviet Union to close transit routes to West Berlin (an island within the centre of the Soviet zone), because the now superfluous old currency would have undermined the economic stability of the East. It was this unilateral action that led directly to the Soviet blockade and the resultant Berlin Airlift.

Even after it came about, the Soviet Union saw the creation of the GDR as a temporary measure with eventual re-unification still the logical outcome. The national anthem of the GDR included the words: 'Arisen from the ruins, looking to the future, let us serve you for the good – Germany, united fatherland'. The Soviet Union actually put forward proposals for unification in 1952 but received a hefty 'no' for an answer from the West German Chancellor Konrad Adenauer. He was an adamant opponent of unification under any circumstances other than under a capitalist system. He famously said that he would 'rather have half of Germany completely than a whole Germany only halfway'. He also said in 1954: 'The best way to regain the German East is rearmament'. And secretly West

Germany was re-armed with the help of the USA.

The Soviet zone of occupation was only a third of German territory, and it was this third that eventually became the GDR. Both that emerging state as well as the policies it pursued were determined by a special combination of circumstances. Throughout that period, its policies could not be separated from those of its 'protector' the USSR; and the fact that it was geographically situated on the front line of the Cold War, also very much determined the course of its history.

There are a whole number of additional reasons why East Germany began life at a great disadvantage when compared with West Germany. In 1945, when the Soviet Army first arrived, the German population had been infected with a visceral hatred and fear of the 'Bolshevik beast' – symbolised in posters, films and articles as an uncultured Asiatic horde, whereas there was little hatred for the USA, Britain or France, despite their also being 'the enemy'. There was certainly no racial hatred towards the Western allies either, as they 'belonged to the Aryan race, unlike the Slavs in the East'. So when the Russians occupied the eastern third of Germany, many Germans had already fled westwards, and those that remained were still imbued with fear and hatred. Before one could begin to build a new Germany, those attitudes had to be neutralised and overcome – an almost insurmountable task.

The East was considerably poorer than its much larger Western counterpart, having little heavy industry and few mineral resources. At war's end it was a territory in ruins. Cities and villages had been devastated even more during the last ditch efforts by the Nazis to halt the advance of the Red Army; tens of thousands were homeless with little available housing and the authorities had to cope with the thousands of refugees from the territories further east, which had now come under Polish or Czech jurisdiction. Most factories had also been bombed and badly damaged.

East Germany found itself largely separated from its traditional western German market as well. It was very dependent on intra-German trade (many raw materials and metals came from the West). But its reliance on intra-German trade was manipulated during the Cold War in an attempt to throttle the GDR's economic revival. Just as an example, in 1951, such trade amounted to 200 million Deutsch Marks, but by 1952 this had dropped to only 9 million.[2]

Furthermore, while large sums under the Marshall Aid Plan were being poured into West Germany, the Soviet Union, in the early years, not only invested nothing in the economy of its zone but actually took out significant sections of the remaining enterprises and infrastructure in reparation for the devastation caused by the Nazis in the Soviet Union.

The starting point for the GDR's economy was therefore far from optimal. More than 2,000 factories were dismantled and transported to the Soviet Union as war reparation payment. This was equivalent to 30 per cent of the industrial capacity in 1944 in that part of Germany. As a comparison, in the Western zones only around 3 per cent was dismantled. Almost 12,000 km of railway track was also removed (equivalent to 48 per cent of the pre-war network). Military industries and those owned by the state or by Nazi activists and war criminals were confiscated by the Soviet Union. These industries represented approximately 60 per cent of total industrial production in the Soviet zone of Germany. It has been estimated that by 1949, 100 per cent of the automotive, between 90-100 per cent of the chemical and 93 per cent of the fuel industries there were in Soviet hands. The Soviet Union also imposed fixed quotas on the renovated factories for goods to be supplied to the Soviet Union (50 per cent of chemical production, 35 per cent of electro-technological products and 25 per cent of all machine tools). In contrast, the FRG received 3.7 billion dollars in Marshall Aid, 15 per cent of which was in the form of a loan and 85 per cent a grant.

US Secretary of State George Marshall, the man behind the programme, floated the idea of economic aid for a devastated Europe in a speech at Harvard University on 5 June 1947. It was vital, he said, to reanimate the moribund economy and reinvigorate societies that were at breaking point. If this were not done quickly, Europe was at risk of turning to communism. This policy would give a vital stimulus to the West German economy. And in 1953, the Western allies signed an agreement with the Federal Republic to write off half its international debts, thus giving another vital boost to its post-war economic recovery.

By 1953, payment of war reparations amounted to 1,349 Reichmarks per capita of population in the GDR whereas in the FRG it was only 23. The renowned West German historian, Arno Peters, calculated that of the hundred billion Deutsch Marks of reparation paid by Germany as a whole to the allies in the wake of the Second World War, 98 per cent was actually paid by East Germany and only 2 per cent by West Germany.[3]

After the 1953 June uprising in the GDR, in response to the government's imposition of new work norms, the Soviet Union began to return the East German factories it had taken in reparations and to provide vital economic support, not least cheap raw materials, including oil.

Politically as well, there was a huge contrast between the GDR and the FRG. If we compare the make-up of the first post war governments in both East and West Germany, there could not be a clearer distinction, and one which very much determined the future politics, attitudes and behaviour of both. Without going into excessive details, below are background sketches of several leading figures from the governments of both East and West.

Many of the leaders of the post-war East German, later GDR, government had a track record of active opposition to the Nazi regime; many had spent years in concentration camps, prison and exile, either in the Soviet Union or in western countries like France, Britain, Mexico or the USA, and a number of them were Jewish. The workers' and socialist movements within Germany had been effectively destroyed by Hitler and many of the leaders had been murdered in concentration camps, and as result there was a limited number of experienced leaders. The inclusion of prominent figures from Jewish backgrounds in the first and subsequent East German governments and in leading positions of the state also serves to undermine the oft-repeated accusation that the GDR was anti-Semitic, and was in stark contrast to the situation in West Germany.[4]

The background of those exiles who returned to East Germany also differed from that of most of the other communist-run countries of Eastern Europe. They returned determined to build a democratic, anti-fascist Germany – that was the intention, and even if those goals were not achieved, fascism was eradicated and an attempt was made, under the most inauspicious circumstances, to build an alternative society to that which had led inexorably to the emergence of fascism.

Otto Grotowohl became the first prime minister of the GDR and an active proponent of a long-lasting peace settlement in Europe. He was the former leader of the Social Democratic Party (SPD) in the Soviet Zone of occupation. He had been imprisoned by the Nazis several times.

Walter Ulbricht, became the first general secretary of the Socialist Unity Party (SED – formed by a merger between the Communist and the Social Democratic Parties in the Soviet Zone in 1946). He was a former joiner, and spent his years of exile in the USSR. He was replaced by Erich Honecker, a former roofer, who became party and state leader after Ulbricht. Honecker had been arrested by the Gestapo in 1935 and spent the following 10 years in a Nazi prison.

Wilhelm Pieck became the first president of the GDR. He had spent the Nazi period and war years in exile in the USSR together with Walter Ulbricht.

Albert Norden, a member of the SED Central Committee, was the son of a Rabbi and had been arrested for political activities during the Weimar Republic, escaping before the Nazis could arrest him and was to spend his exile years in the USA.

Herman Axen, a member of the Central Committee, came from a Jewish family and survived internment in both Auschwitz and Buchenwald.

Klaus Gysi, later Minister of Culture, also came from a Jewish family background and escaped the Nazis to spend his exile working with the resistance in France and Britain.

Markus Wolf, who became the GDR's head of counter espionage, came from a Jewish background. He was the son of the renowned playwright and medical doctor Friedrich Wolf . He was also in the Soviet Union during the Nazi period.

Rudolph Herrnstadt came from a Jewish family and spent the Nazi and war years in Soviet exile. He became the first chief editor of *Neues Deutschland*, the national daily newspaper of the SED.

Alexander Abusch, the first Minister of Culture, was born to a Jewish family in Cracow and spent the war years in French exile.

Hilde Benjamin, also from a Jewish background, became the GDR's first female minister and its second Minister of Justice. Under the Nazis she had been banned from practising law because of her Jewish background. She was the wife of Dr. Georg Benjamin (brother of the writer and cultural critic Walter Benjamin) who was murdered in Mauthausen concentration camp. She was instrumental in bringing in a whole raft of legislation favouring gender equality in the GDR.

In West Germany, Konrad Adenauer became the first post-war Chancellor. He was an arch-conservative, ardent Catholic and pre-war mayor of Cologne as well as President of the Prussian State Council. Before the war he had called for a coalition government with the Nazis, and although never a member of that party himself, he was certainly no anti-fascist. His first post war government was packed with other right-wing and conservative Catholic figures as well as high-ranking former Nazis.

Hans Globke was Adenauer's personal advisor. He had been an active member of the Nazi party, and had served as chief legal advisor to the Office for Jewish Affairs in the Ministry of the Interior, the section headed by Adolf Eichmann that was responsible for the administrative logistics of the Holocaust. It was he who co-wrote the official annotation explaining the implementation of the race laws which legalised the discrimination against the Jews.

West Germany's second Chancellor, Ludwig Erhard, the man credited with the country's post-war 'economic miracle' and dubbed the 'father of the social market economy' had previously occupied a leading position in the Nazi Reichsgruppe Industrie and the Institute for Industrial Research financed by the chemical conglomerate IG Farben that supplied Zyklon-B for the gas chambers.

Kurt Kiesinger, who followed Erhard as Chancellor in 1966, joined the Nazi Party in 1933, a few weeks after Hitler came to power. In 1940, he was employed in the Ministry of Foreign Affairs' radio propaganda department, rising to become deputy head from 1943 to 1945 and was liaison officer with Goebbels' Ministry of Propaganda.

Heinrich Lübke, who became President of the Federal Republic in 1959, was another controversial figure. His signature (which he disputed) was found on the building plans for a concentration camp. He was involved in the setting up of an aircraft factory in an underground chamber and, under his direction, barracks were built to house concentration camp inmates who worked as slave labourers. Lübke was also involved in setting up the army research station at Peenemunde (where the V2 rockets were developed under Werner von Braun) as building director of the Schlemp Group. From 1943-45 he was responsible for the employment of concentration camp inmates as slave labour.

Hans Speidel, Commander-in-Chief of the allied ground forces in Central Europe from 1957 to 1963, served in the Nazi army's French campaign of 1940 and became Chief of Staff of the military commander in France. In April 1944, Speidel was appointed Chief of Staff to Field Marshall Rommel.

Reinhard Gehlen, President of the BND, the West German secret service until 1968, had been chief of Hitler's military intelligence unit on the Eastern Front. He had been officially released from American captivity in 1946 and flown back to Germany, where he began his intelligence work by setting up an organization of former German intelligence officers.

Only when Willi Brandt, who first became Mayor of West Berlin (1957-66), became German Chancellor (1969-74), was there a genuine anti-fascist at the helm of the Federal Republic. He had spent the exile years in Norway working as a journalist and hiding from the Nazis. For many years he was ostracised by establishment figures in West Germany as a 'traitor', just as Marlene Dietrich and others who left Germany during the Hitler years were. It was perhaps not surprising that it was only under Brandt's Chancellorship that a thaw in East-West relations began to take place with a tentative rapprochement between the GDR and FRG.

Right into the 1960s, many highly decorated Nazis and war criminals were occupying top positions within the West German state. There were 21 Secretaries of State and ministers, 100 generals and admirals in the Bundeswehr, 825 senior members of the judiciary, 245 leading civil servants in the diplomatic corps and foreign service who had been top Nazis. Many senior lawyers who had willingly enacted Nazi laws and handed down death sentences for political 'crimes', and medical professionals who had been involved in inhuman experimentation, race hygiene, genetic selection, forced sterilisations and euthanasia, were reinstated.

Jutta Ditfurth writes in her autobiography that there were a series of trials of former Nazis during the fifties in the FRG but the fact that 'individual jurists, among them state prosecutors, felt strengthened in their determination to prosecute was as a result of the international pressure exerted internationally by the GDR with its publicising information about the so-called West German "judges with blood on their hands".' She gives the example of the psychiatrist Dr. Carl Schneider, who had been involved in the Nazis' euthanasia programme, but after 1945, became director of Heidelberg University's psychiatric clinic.[5]

This background and the way prominent personalities rose to power in the divided post-war Germany demonstrate that while in the East a genuine de-nazification process did take place, in the West it was desultory to begin with and later non-existent: many leading Nazis merely donned the new 'democratic' clothing and continued to occupy or re-occupy influential positions. Apart from the handful of top Nazis convicted at the Nuremberg trials, very few were called to account for their roles during the Nazi period.[6] In fact, in the early post-war period the USA put a stop to any further attempts to bring Nazis to trial because it was determined to focus on its anti-communist crusade. It was felt that a continued pursuance of Nazis would hinder that aim and alienate its vital German ally.

Writers and artists like Bertolt Brecht, Anna Seghers, Marlene Dietrich and even Thomas Mann were told that by fleeing Hitler they had betrayed the 'German spirit' and the 'German soul' and were not welcome in West Germany. Thomas Mann feared for his life in Germany 'without the protection of the allies' bayonets'. 'Monopoly capital' which found the highest expression of its dominance under fascism 'is prepared for a fight to the death and to countenance any crime before it relinquishes its position'. With reference to the process of de-nazification, he commented that in the industrial centre of the Ruhr, 'the old men and those who financed Hitler have been installed once again, as governors of American capital.'[7] Mann sought refuge in Switzerland.

While the GDR might not have been the epitome of democracy, neither was the Federal Republic. Both were scarred and marred by the post-war settlement, but in radically different ways. In 1950, Adenauer banned all communists from public service, and in 1956 outlawed the Communist Party of Germany (KPD), the Free German Youth organisation (FDJ), the Federation of Victims of Fascism (VVN) and the German-Soviet Friendship Society (DSFS), while protecting and reinstating former Nazis.

In 1951, a special amendment to the constitution (Ausführungs-Gesetz zu Artikel 131 des Grundgesetzes) was passed by the Bundestag which marked the conclusion of this process. The law gave everyone, apart from the few notorious Nazi leaders, the right to return to their posts in the public service. Similar laws were passed in all the regions, as in Schleswig Holstein, with its 'Law on the ending of de-nazification' (Gesetz zur Beendigung der Entnazifizierung on 31 Januar 1951). This meant in effect that the legal prosecution of former Nazis would no longer be pursued. However, the persecution of communists continued, with arrests and imprisonment – they became the political prisoners the West German government never acknowledged.

By the mid-1960s, around 250,000 judicial investigations had been undertaken against suspected communists and around 10,000 were actually imprisoned as were socialists and others opposed to a remilitarisation of the country or who were members of organisations working to promote links of friendship with the GDR.[8] A big demonstration in May 1952 for peace and against the remilitarisation of Germany, was banned by the West German government. Despite this, thousands converged on the city of Essen, but were violently attacked by the police using live ammunition and dogs. Many young people were badly injured and three were shot in the back, one of whom later died of his wounds.[8]

It is interesting to note, that the Federal Republic never formally accepted the post-war settlement and Germany's new borders to the east. The GDR, the furthermost eastern part of post-war Germany, was invariably referred to as 'Mitteldeutschland' or Middle Germany, particularly in the right-wing press, a tacit refusal to recognise the post-war settlement, which had ceded eastern Prussia to Poland.

There were also powerful organisations of 'Landsmannschaften' (homeland associations) in West Germany that demanded the return of the lost territories in the East – East Prussia, Silesia, Bohemia, Danzig, Sudetenland – or defended the right of those Germans expelled after the war to return. They refused to accept the post war settlement or the new borders, and received considerable support from Conservative politicians and tacit support from the government.

Those who had spent the war years in exile or in Nazi concentration camps and who returned to East Germany to help rebuild the devastated country were totally inexperienced in government or in wielding power. They were idealists full of hope and with dreams of building a different Germany. They had no firm plans or even a route map. Much had to be improvised as a reaction to events or to actions taken by the West. They certainly had no intention of attempting to create a separate German state on the territory of only a third of the country. When it became the GDR and proclaimed its aim as the building of socialism, its enemies predicted it would only survive a few months before collapsing and did everything they could to assist that process. Throughout its existence the GDR found itself in a permanent state of siege and subject to an economic war, not unlike that suffered by Cuba.

Very much as a result of large-scale foreign, mainly US, investment in the early post-war period, West Germany soon recovered its pre-war economic eminence; its population was again soon enjoying relatively high standards of living. The GDR, as its poorer neighbour, found itself haemorrhaging qualified workers and professionals through its open border with the West in Berlin. Many were not fleeing communist persecution, but simply voting with their feet for higher salaries and a wider range of consumer goods on offer in the West. And they could all expect to find jobs immediately because, according to the West German constitution, they were not classed as migrants but were deemed to be citizens of the Federal Republic. In other words, and this was unique in the world in terms of inter-state relationships, GDR citizens only needed to enter the Federal Republic to immediately and automatically receive citizenship and state support. They were provided with West German papers and passports, helped to find housing and jobs.

The Federal Republic never officially recognised the GDR, so this made it easy and attractive for people to move west. Most were classic economic migrants looking for a better life. Annual emigration increased from an estimated figure of around 143,000 in 1959 to 199,000 in 1960, one year before the Wall was built. The majority of these were white collar and professional workers and 50 per cent were under 25 years of age. In 1960 alone, 688 doctors, 296 dentists and 2,648 engineers went to the West.[10]

The labour and brain drain exceeded a total of 2.5 million citizens between 1949 and 1961, when the Wall was built. In addition, the open border in Berlin was a focus of Cold War tensions and on a number of occasions events threatened to take the two military blocks to war. It was also a Mecca for spies and for acts of sabotage against the GDR. There is little doubt, even in the minds of those who were very much opposed to the GDR, that the building of the Wall in August 1961 contributed to reducing tensions. Clearly, though, the GDR's main reason for building it was to stem the drain of skilled personnel as well as to exercise proper control over its own borders, just like any other state. As a direct result of the Wall being built the economy could be stabilised and made more viable; but at the same time many people, particularly in Berlin, resented the feeling of being cut off from West Germany.

Right from the date of its foundation on 7 October 1949, there was a determination in the West, but particularly on the part of the Federal Republic, to 'strangle it at birth', to ensure that an alternative social model to Western capitalism would not survive. Various kinds of chicanery were used to make life for the GDR impossible, including sabotage.[11] The Federal Republic claimed to be the only legitimate German state and to represent all Germans.

During the first 20 years of its existence, the GDR was unable to establish diplomatic relations with countries outside the 13 Communist bloc states because of the Hallstein Doctrine, named after Walter Hallstein, the West German politician and academic. In effect, it hindered other countries establishing diplomatic relations with the GDR and it would not maintain diplomatic relations with any state that recognised it. The FRG also exercised enormous pressure on all states that even considered establishing diplomatic or trading ties with the GDR.

Egypt was the first non-socialist country to recognise the GDR in 1965. Despite the Federal Republic granting the country aid to the tune of around 1.4 billion Deutsch Marks in order to keep it on board, its new leader, Abdul el-Nasser, decided to recognise the GDR. His action caused dismay in Bonn. Spiegel magazine wrote, 'nowhere has the Hallstein doctrine been more costly for us than in Egypt'.[12]When GDR Prime Minister Walter Ulbricht planned to visit Egypt shortly after recognition, all western nations under the projected flight path refused permission for his plane to fly over their territory, so he was obliged to fly to Yugoslavia and take a boat. Such was the chicanery and the petty vindictiveness of the Cold War.

The young GDR had been very dependent on its traditional trading links with western Germany and on supply and export contracts. Such links were made increasingly difficult, with western firms coming under political pressure to sever trading relations; contracts were suddenly and arbitrarily terminated in attempts to disrupt manufacturing recovery in the GDR.

The GDR had no raw materials apart from lignite, potash and uranium, so was reliant on imports. Without raw materials an establishment of a manufacturing industry and economic development was impossible. The Federal Republic instituted a steel export embargo in 1950 and a complete ban on intra-German trade in 1951, including anthracite coal upon which the GDR was reliant. These were only some of the methods of chicanery used to prevent GDR development.

In the immediate post-war years and the early years after the founding of the GDR a concerted policy of peaceful coexistence and anti-militarism was pursued. Even military toys were banned and young people educated to work for peace in the world.[13] The Soviet Union regularly requested the signing of a peace treaty with the Federal Republic but was rebuffed by Chancellor Adenauer. Such a peace treaty was never signed and the FRG never formally recognised the post-war Oder-Neisse border between Germany and Poland.

When it became clear that the West German government, in conjunction with the USA, was determined to remilitarise and join NATO, the GDR and the Soviet Union changed their policy of seeking a permanent post-war peaceful settlement. On 12 November 1955 the FRG set up the Bundeswehr (West German armed forces) and re-introduced universal compulsory military service in 1956. The GDR felt obliged to respond and established the Volksarmee (GDR People's Army) on 1 March 1956; for the first six years it was an all-volunteer force.

A MORE EGALITARIAN SOCIETY

One of the greatest achievements of the GDR was the establishment and maintenance of a more egalitarian society. Pre-war Germany, like all western societies, had been characterised by class privilege. The top echelons of government, the diplomatic service, medicine, judiciary and academia had been dominated by the upper and middle classes. Women had been largely confined to their traditional domestic and low-paid roles.

The GDR immediately began introducing a series of measures to counter this class and gender privilege and increase the educational and career prospects of working class children (this is explained in more detail later). This was highly successful and the GDR became one of the most egalitarian societies in Europe. Full gender equality and equal pay were enshrined in legislation. Pay differentials between different groups of employees were minimal, so that even top managers or government ministers were not wealthy in Western terms, although they did enjoy a rather more privileged existence and higher pay than their office cleaner. Average pay differentials in the GDR were 1:3 whereas in the Federal Republic they were 1:20.

Even in terms of housing, economic and class difference played little role. All residential areas contained a mix of professional and working class people. Interestingly, despite all the vilifying of the former communist world, few pundits have attempted to provide evidence that the former leaders or party officials amassed inordinate wealth, or had their own private mansions, as all despots and business-owners in the capitalist world have done.[14] This lack of large wealth differentials, class privilege and ghettoisation made for a much more cohesive and balanced society devoid of the sort of tensions we find in the West. In their book, *The Spirit Level – Why More Equal Societies Almost Always Do Better*, Wilkinson and Pickett demonstrate clearly how income inequalities are one of the main causes of social ills. And, undoubtedly, in the GDR a more egalitarian distribution of wealth made for a healthier and more balanced society. For some, of course, such egalitarianism was not amenable, and the lure of higher salaries and business opportunities in the West remained strong.

As the GDR became more established and accepted as a separate and sovereign state as well as an economic force, its citizens also developed a new self-assuredness, largely as a result of the guaranteed social stability and sense of security. They were very much aware of their indispensible role in the whole social structure. They had guaranteed security of employment, housing at regulated rents, a free health service and other free or inexpensive social services. It was virtually impossible to fall through the social net. On the other hand, because the state had successfully removed existential fears, at the same time, it set free social energies and aspirations that went beyond the mere basic needs of life. Precisely because life-threatening insecurity in the workplace and in society had been largely eliminated, people became relaxed enough to undertake experimentation on a personal level, indulging in non-traditional thinking and taking on more open and spontaneous ways of living. And exactly that was what made the party and state authorities uncomfortable.[14]

In schools, the better pupils helped those less able and class achievements were seen as equally important as one's own individual attainments. A sense of pride grew in achievements of the school class, the school itself or the state – they were things everyone had contributed towards and of which they could be proud.

In the factories, the brigade or team system helped engender the idea of co-operation and better working together. Brigades would also socialise outside work and celebrate joint successes with a social get-together in a local restaurant, a group trip to the theatre, exhibitions or sporting events. The majority of people were encouraged to think and behave in terms of promoting the good of society and not simply their own individual advancement or wealth.

Society was more united and social cohesion much stronger than in many Western societies. The lack of focussed consumer pressures on children, young people or women also helped maintain this cohesiveness. The young were not pitted against the old, women were not discriminated against in terms of their social roles. The tendency in capitalist countries of companies to target specific groups in order to exploit a niche market leads invariably to a more divided society and fractured relationships.

Social ethos – the community spirit

'I didn't love the GDR, but I was happy living in the GDR'. That was what a former GDR citizen told former prime minister Hans Modrow. It probably sums up the attitude of many GDR citizens who disliked aspects of the way the country was run and the oppressive dominance of the leading party, but who valued the social ethos prevalent in the country.

The social ethos in the GDR laid emphasis on solidarity, mutual help and support. Everyone was encouraged to feel responsibility in some way for what happened around them. This meant that serious crime and anti-social behaviour were minimal. In general, people had no fears of being out on the streets late at night or entering particular areas of a city; women, too, were not subjected to the levels of sexual harassment they often endure in capitalist countries. Not that such things did not happen, they did, but were exceptions.

In Western societies, dominated by a free-market ideology, we have seen a breakdown of communities, of solidarity and mutual care. When prime minister Margaret Thatcher notoriously announced that 'there is no such thing as society', and set about proving it, individuals were encouraged to become more self-centred; solidarity was deemed to be an old fashioned and retrogressive concept. She did this by implementing policies which, among other things, forced local councils to sell off social housing and by hobbled the trade unions. Our society is now ridden with fears – of crime, unemployment, homelessness and isolation.

Children were generally seen as everyone's responsibility. Typically, you could see a row of prams in front of a shop or department store with sleeping babies. If one of them woke up while their mothers or fathers were inside shopping, passers-by would often interact with the child, trying to calm it down if it was distressed, until the parents returned. Fully qualified staff in schools and nurseries ensured children were well cared for and educationally stimulated. Neighbours, too, took an interest in and were concerned about children's wellbeing. There were thus very few cases of abuse, abandonment, delinquency or serious mental health problems as a result of lack of care.

It is that sense of community that was very strong in the GDR. People did not just live alongside each other, they interacted with each other. Germans (East and West) tend to live in blocks of flats more than in individual houses, and in the GDR the majority of flats belonged to the communities and some were owned by co-operatives. The social mix in these blocks of flats was very different from anything one would find in the UK or in the new Germany. There were academics living next to craftsmen, teachers next to train drivers, civil servants next to shop assistants. This is also the reason why living in a flat was not seen as a 'second choice' – they were the typical mode of accommodation and everybody was keen to make their block and the surroundings as pleasant as possible.

Tenants themselves were responsible for the cleaning of the communal areas: the corridors, staircases, airing and washing rooms in the cellar and other communal areas.

Where applicable, tenants also took responsibility for caring for the surrounding outside areas which could include lawns, shrubbery and flowerbeds. In winter, they were responsible for clearing snow from the pavement fronting their blocks. Tenants shared this work and took turns on a rota basis. In order to organise the rotas and manage the sums paid by the local authority for the carrying out of this necessary communal work, so-called 'Hausgemeinschaften' (residents' associations in each block of flats) were formed.

These associations varied in size depending on the number of flats. Some associations were very active and organised group visits to the theatre or held parties; others just did the minimum. It very much depended on the people living in the block; there was no outside pressure. The money received for looking after the public areas of the flats was held in a common fund. This fund was also supplemented by monies received from recycling.

Recycling was a big thing in the GDR. Already in the 1950s, there was regular recycling of bottles, jars and paper. Back then it was not so much for environmental reasons but because of a scarcity of raw materials and therefore there was an urgent need to make the best use of the available material. However the habit of recycling stuck, and later, when public concerns about the environment became more central, the number of items that could be recycled was expanded. For instance, plastic and batteries were already being recycled in the 1980s. Recycling was easy in the GDR because there were many small, local recycling stations within walking distance – and people were reimbursed for items recycled. For both these reasons it worked well.

Everybody recycled, including children who were encouraged in school and by the Young Pioneers organisation. While some collected bottles and paper to earn extra money for themselves, others did it in order to raise money for a particular project. Women and pensioner organisations were involved, as were allotment associations. While these had special recycling campaigns, tenant associations were the key for regular recycling. Many collected all items to be recycled in a special room in the basement of their block of flats and then organised appropriate transport to the nearest recycling station. Some even had contracts with factories and delivered bottles to them directly for re-use.

The residents' association in a block of flats decided how to use the money that had been built up in their fund over the year. Some created a hobby room with DIY tools, some a special storage space for bicycles or even a party room that could be used by all tenants; some organised parties specially for children or for all the tenants; other associations paid out to every tenant a percentage of the money at the end of the year. How the money was used was democratically decided in the association. This carrying out of community work together and holding parties helped tenants get to know each other really well, and this also encouraged mutual support when it was needed.

Equal rights for women

In the GDR, the idea of emancipation was based on the political struggles going back to the 19th century when August Bebel (1840-1913) and Clara Zetkin (1857-1933) argued that the solution of the 'women's question' was inextricably linked with a liberation from exploitation and the creation of a socialist society.

Equal rights for women were anchored in the constitution from the very beginning of the GDR. The 1949 constitution states simply: 'Men and women are equal.' In 1950, the GDR introduced a specific law (Gesetz über die Rechte der Frau) with the aim of securing the rights of women and protecting mothers. It stated that 'marriage must not result in a reduction of women's rights'. It emphasised the need for support in training and professional development for women and made any dismissal because of pregnancy illegal. The reasoning behind this law was given as making 'it possible for women to take part in creative work for society, in local and national government, in political as well as cultural areas in both towns and villages'.

The law of 1950 guaranteed not only financial support for mothers; crucially, it gave single mothers the same rights as married ones. In contrast, even as late as the 1990s, single mothers in the Republic of Ireland were being punished because of the influence and political dominance, of the Catholic Church.

The same law also demanded the commissioning and building of medical centres for children as well as the setting up of children's wards in hospitals. Thousands of full-time nursery and kindergarten places were created. As a result, women in the GDR embarked on a broad variety of professions and trades, were economically independent, had a high level of self-confidence and provided very different images of and for women compared to the West.

Further rights for women were granted under a new law that came into force in 1965, initiated by the first female Secretary of State for Justice, Hilde Benjamin. This gave women the right to develop their own career paths through training and qualification. It also simplified the regulations regarding divorce, abolishing the notion of guilt and replacing it with the 'break-up principle', e.g. if a husband attempted to prevent his wife following her own career choices. In contrast, in the Federal Republic, up until 1976, men were the sole owners of property, had the sole legal right in terms of decision-making regarding children, and a married woman was only able to work with the permission of her husband and 'if her domestic duties did not suffer as a result.'

Women in the FRG tended to stay at home once they started a family with the result that only 50 per cent of all women worked. Those in the FRG who had children, tended to work part-time and many who worked full-time did not have children.

The professional development of women was achieved by the creation of a generous support system for women who were aiming to gain qualifications. Programmes for the advancement of women were developed and special study programmes were introduced at technical colleges and universities. There were also courses that allowed a combination of work and study, with three days a week work and two days of study at a guaranteed 90 per cent of salary.[16]

Childcare support improved steadily and as early as 1961 employment legislation was introduced that stipulated criteria for the improvement of childcare support for single mothers and fathers at times when their children were ill and introduced the concept of a 'baby year' (i.e. a year off work). This was, initially, unpaid (apart from the maternity pay of 90 per cent for 14 weeks) but came with a job guarantee.

1972 was an important year for the emancipation of women in the GDR. Abortion was made legal and free contraception became available for all women above the age of 16. Maternity leave, paid at 90 per cent of salary, was increased from 14 to 18 weeks (to be increased to 26 weeks in 1976). In addition, the payment of 1,000 Marks (more than a month's average salary) was introduced on the birth of a baby as support for the parents. Furthermore, young couples under the age of 26 were granted interest-free loans of 5,000 Marks.

In 1976, a whole year on full pay following the birth of the second child was introduced as a right. From 1980, the 'baby year' was paid for every child and, crucially, could be shared between mother and father. There was also a no-redundancy clause for single mothers.

Important and helpful was the fact that parents were paid their full wages for up to four weeks per year for looking after a child that had fallen ill. This removed the pressure on parents and avoided the need for parents to send children back to nursery before they were fully recovered in order to ensure a steady income.

Being in work was a normal part of life for women; it brought economic independence, self-confidence and the feeling of being part of society and not just the family. Women in the GDR did not just take part in the economic process, they were well qualified (81 per cent of all working women had a qualification for the work they were doing) and had careers in all walks of life, not just in traditional 'women's jobs'. They also felt more liberated because separation and divorce were relatively easy, not least because they rarely involved property share-outs. And partnerships that did not involve formal marriage were also quite widespread.

Because of women's new sense of freedom from the worries about the costs of bringing up children and funding their care, the birth rate in the GDR was healthy – unlike in the Federal Republic where it soon fell below the population replacement rate. Most young women in the GDR could and did choose to have children and work at the same time.

After only 20 years of the GDR's existence, 34 per cent of judges in the GDR were women (in the FRG 6 per cent) and by 1988, this figure had increased to more than 50 per cent, and one third of women worked in technical professions.[17] At the same time, women in the GDR held the post of mayor in 1,172 towns and villages (out of 9,021); in contrast, in the FRG, there were only 12 women mayors (out of a total of 14,869 towns and villages). It is perhaps essential to note here that 'mayors' in Germany are the leading local administrative officials not, as in Britain, merely ceremonial figures.[18]

While the above figures for women's participation in society and the workplace are indeed impressive by any standards, it has to be admitted that in the very top echelons of society i.e. in the Party hierarchy, in government and top factory management, women's representation was almost as unsatisfactory as in many Western countries at the time.

One other aspect of life in the GDR, which had a particularly positive impact on women and their sense of self worth, but which is often neglected, was the absence of mass advertising. Cynics would argue that the country had no advertising because it had no consumer goods worth advertising. While it is true that there was not a superfluity of goods that needed advertising to sell them, there was also a conscious determination not to encourage consumerism as an end in itself. This, of course, meant that women were not continually confronted with impossible role models to aspire to in terms of physical beauty or possessions, and their sexuality was not exploited for promoting sales. Rather than the plethora of women's magazine stacked high on newsagents' shelves in the West, with their never-ending fashion and cosmetics tips and cooking recipes, in the GDR women readers were treated as normally intelligent and independent beings with a broad spectrum of interests.

The most widely-read women's magazine, *Für Dich*, had a circulation of almost a million. Not only were all the journalists working for it, including the editor, women, the stories they featured were about women of the present and the past, of women at work, women artists or sportswomen. Women in the GDR were thus able to navigate society as individuals, on a par with men, and had no pressures on them to conform to any advertiser's fantasy of the dream woman.

Even after 25 years of unification women in the East still have a very different self-perception of their role. They do not accept the traditional role model still prevalent in the West of a man as chief breadwinner and the married woman only working to supplement his income. Women in the East want to work and have a family – as they had known it. Work for women means independence as the most important basis for equality. Work is seen as significant not only for the individual but also because it provides a sense of belonging and of contributing to a larger social entity.

Childcare

The GDR had arguably one of the best childcare systems in the world. A comprehensive system of childcare was introduced very early on, including crèches (for babies up to the age of three), nurseries (for children aged three to six) and after-school care (for primary school children).

This system was vital in enabling women to embark on careers outside the home and explains why 91 per cent of all women of childbearing age opted to have children. The nurseries and kindergartens were run by trained professionals, who provided the children with a stimulating and age-appropriate educational input. They were an important aspect in the vital socialisation of children.

By 1989, anyone who wanted to have a place in a nursery was able to obtain one – either in their community or in the workplace. And for 80 per cent of babies and toddlers, there were crèches available. The universal availability of childcare meant that women were able to continue in their profession or trade after maternity leave. Due to the fact that work and school in the GDR began at 7 am, nurseries opened as early as 6 am and generally closed at 6 pm. Children would be brought to the nursery at different times depending on their parents' work pattern, and usually stayed about seven or eight hours. Nurseries were basically free of charge with parents only paying a small contribution towards food.

Primary schools which, like all schools in Germany, finished their day at lunchtime, stayed open in the afternoons and offered a secure and supervised place for children to do their homework and play before their parents returned home from work. Children were also given nutritious meals at school or nursery during the day, to ensure an adequate and healthy diet. During the school holidays, supervised activities for children were organised in the schools and Pioneer centres (The Young Pioneers was the national organisation for younger children).

Real emancipation cannot be measured simply by how many women are represented in the boardrooms or heading up business organisations, but through the living and working conditions of the majority of women. This is underlined by a report written by a West German journalist in 1971. He spent ten weeks in the GDR filming for ARD television. There he conducted in-depth interviews with two families and arrived at a well-nigh euphoric viewpoint as far as GDR women and GDR families were concerned. Even the career training of the women he talked to seemed to him to be remarkable. One had qualified as a chemical technician and then gained a further qualification as a team leader. The other was a qualified instructor and had just completed her chemical engineering diploma. His comment: 'Socialism doesn't destroy the family. But with its development of women as people, as people in society, the family changes and will do so with increasing speed in the GDR, so that by the year 2000 it will have little resemblance to the old style family...'[19]

Young people

Every effort was made by the GDR leadership to involve young people in the building of the socialist state. After all, they would be the first generation not to have experienced the Nazi era and their minds would be free of its insidious ideology. It was hoped that through a different type of education, the anchoring of socialist norms and the engendering of a sense of loyalty to the state, a new generation of committed socialists would emerge. And, indeed, in a new state with a massive shortage of labour, expertise and experience, young people had enormous opportunities, albeit within the limits of a relatively small country. Youth centres were established in every locality, sports facilities were widespread and usage was completely free.

Traditional gender discrimination in schools, universities and in the professions was abolished and women were given special encouragement and incentives to gain higher qualifications. This led to a significant increase in girls taking up and qualifying at higher levels in traditional male subjects, like maths, engineering and the natural sciences.

Every pupil who left school, if they did not go on to higher education, would be offered apprenticeship training. There was a widespread system of vocational training schools in which students could study and learn a trade as well as continue their general education during a three-year course and for that period received a grant.

Youth initiatives were encouraged and schemes such as the 'Exhibition by the Masters of Tomorrow' (Messe der Meister von Morgen or MMM) were established to foster innovation by young people in the fields of technology and science and as a motivation for young people to take on responsibilities in society. The MMM was first initiated in 1958 and it became an annual event. It started out at school and factory level, where the best ideas, inventions, innovations and projects were developed before being passed on to the district and later regional level where the very best would be selected and exhibited in Leipzig. Many thousands took part. For example, in 1982, a collective developed the idea of using methane gas as a substitute for petrol to be used in vehicles. The invention was presented at the MMM and later actually implemented by industry.

Young people were given every encouragement to achieve the highest educational attainments, to undertake career training and partake in political, leisure and sports activities. The organisation of Young Pioneers, named after Ernst Thälmann (the communist leader murdered by the Nazis) and the youth organisation, Free German Youth (FDJ), undertook much of this work. Almost all school children, aged six to thirteen, belonged to the Young Pioneer organisation while the FDJ was for young people aged 14 to 26 years of age.

Among the principles in the credo of the young pioneers were: 'we love our parents, our country and peace; we aim to learn and work hard at school; we help one another; we are active in sports, enjoy singing and dancing'. Young pioneers had various projects that often included tending particular public spaces, improving and making them attractive. These projects might include memorial sites, public parks but also helping older and vulnerable people. The idea was to encourage young children to become aware of their environment and take some responsibility for it.

Young pioneers would also put on concerts for older people, do shopping for them, help collect materials to be recycled and gather winter feed for wild animals.

They had their own cultural centres and venues where they could pursue their individual interests, from model-making, playing musical instruments, dancing or singing, in a less formal environment than at school. There were also holiday camps for young pioneers as well as special centres for young technical experts and those interested in the natural world.

The FDJ, which had been set up as an anti-fascist youth movement and played a central role after the war in the re-education of young people, was more overtly political and suited to an older age group. It was the only officially recognised national youth organisation and most young people belonged to it. However, those of a strongly religious persuasion often joined the church youth organisiation, Junge Gemeinde (Young Congregation).

The FDJ has been universally characterised in the West as an organisation for indoctrinating young people along the lines of the Hitler Youth, but in the ideology of Marxism. Although it was guided by the state and was seen as a means of educating young people in the ethos of socialism, its overall aims were humanistic and it promoted the ideas of international solidarity, co-operation and social responsibility.

The FDJ had its own national newspaper, *Junge Welt* (Young World) and was represented as the official student voice in schools and colleges, and it also had representatives in Parliament. Many learned how to organise events, practise public speaking and, through the activities of the FDJ, had the opportunity of meeting others outside their own sphere of experience. It organised, for instance, national and international festivals where young people from different countries would meet. It was instrumental in developing the modern folk song movement with its annual festivals in Berlin. FDJ members took part in international assistance programmes in aid of other countries such as Nicaragua, Mozambique and Angola, supporting vital projects there. The FDJ was also involved in large, ongoing projects, the biggest of which was the construction of a huge pipeline across the Soviet Union that would transport gas from the Soviet Union to the other socialist countries.

Another interesting and significant innovation introduced in the GDR was the Jugendweihe (which can be very roughly translated as a secular or humanist confirmation or coming-of-age celebration). The concept of a secular coming-of age-ceremony can be traced back to the Freethinkers and the Age of Enlightenment, and gained in popularity among secular groups during the 19th century as an alternative to confirmation by the Catholic and Protestant churches. It was reintroduced in the GDR as a secular alternative and became a significant day of celebration for young people entering adulthood.

In preparation for the Jugendweihe ceremony, schools would organise events on specific topics in order to help prepare young people for adulthood, including discussions on German history (often combined with a visit to one of the Nazi concentration camps), on rights and responsibilities under socialism and what contribution each individual can make to society, the importance of art and culture (often including visits to galleries, museums and theatres) as well as the role of science and technology in human progress. The central idea was that young people, through the Jugendweihe ceremony, would be formally accepted as young adults. This was expressed through the fact that the celebrant would from then on have to be addressed using the formal 'Sie' rather than the 'Du' used for children. While the celebration was initially viewed dubiously, it soon became popular and by the 1960s almost all 14 year-olds participated. This secular ceremony is still carried out widely today, mainly in the eastern parts of Germany.

Despite the emphasis placed on young people's contribution to society, however, the GDR was no exception to the general rule that young people, by their very nature, are rebellious, ready to kick against constraints and restrictions, rejecting adult perceptions of how the world should be. So although the Party made quite amazing progress in rallying large numbers of young people to its banner, there were also considerable numbers – particularly in the later years – who were chafing at the bit and increasingly rejected the central controlling role of the Party, demanding more democracy and freedom.

The pioneer organisation was dissolved just before unification and the FDJ haemorrhaged members, not least because it is still a banned organisation in Germany. As early as 1951, the organisation had been made illegal in West Germany because, with its appeals to halt the country's rearmament, it was deemed to be subverting the constitution.

With the destruction of the GDR's economic base, post unification, there was a huge loss of jobs and many youth centres and sports clubs were closed or privatised. As a result, many young people felt abandoned and disorientated. In view of the sudden collapse of the system that young people had grown up with and the accompanying denigration of all it stood for, it is, perhaps, little wonder that scores of young people in the former GDR have been attracted to right wing extremist groups with their seductive 'easy' answers, especially in view of the ensuing rise in unemployment and lack of opportunity for them in the new Germany.

Social wage

Wage differentials were minimal and the difference between a low earner and high earner was nowhere near as vast as in the West. Pay levels in general were not very high compared to western standards but living costs were much lower, and personal income was supplemented by what was called the 'social wage'. Profits created by the publicly owned enterprises went into the social pot and were used to improve life for everyone – not just for a few owners or shareholders who would pocket the surplus. The social wage meant that essential items, such as food, rent, public transport and children's clothing were heavily subsidised and thus made affordable for everyone; it also allowed for subsidies on cultural and leisure activities to make them accessible for all.

Every newly married couple under 26 received an interest-free loan from the state to help them set up a home. With the birth of each child, mothers received the equivalent of one month's average wages to buy essential items for the child. The impact on individuals and families of such state subsidies, apart from their social value, cannot be overstated. The idea of a social wage is a vital concept for any society purporting to be egalitarian. It was instrumental in ensuring the implementation of greater social equality, undermining privilege and class hegemony. However, such subsidies also created problems. Over time, fixed and stable prices for rents, public transport, energy and similar items took an increasing amount out of the state purse. The problems were not the subsidies themselves but the inflexible adherence to those prices even though raw material costs and wages had increased.[20]

It was difficult to buy a car in the GDR and there was a very long waiting list – but this did not mean people were unable to travel. The railway system, buses and trams were efficient, regular and cheap, including in the rural areas where there was a comprehensive and regular bus service. In the towns, subsidised public transport could be used for a flat rate of 20 Pfennigs (approx. 10 pence) operating on a trust basis, and even though checks were rare, almost everyone did pay. Owning one's own personal means of transport was a luxury that not everyone by far could afford, but few really needed.

Although most people in the GDR lived in rented accommodation (at controlled and affordable rents – typically five per cent of one's income), a considerable minority owned their own houses and some (often craftsmen, small business people, but also workers) built their own privately owned houses. There was not much incentive to own one's own home in the GDR as rents were cheap because they were subsidised and security of tenure guaranteed by law. Even so, between 11,000 and 12,000 privately owned homes were built annually during the 1980s.[21] In order to support this, generous loans at very low interest rates were often granted by the state.

Rent levels remained virtually unchanged throughout the life of the GDR and no one could be evicted from their home. The war had left an acute housing shortage, and throughout its history the GDR fought to overcome the lack of decent housing. In 1973, Erich Honecker, after his election as General Secretary of the Socialist Unity Party, announced a massive house-building programme as 'a core aspect of social policy' and promised that by 1990 'housing as a social problem would be a thing of the past.'[22] Between 100,000 and 110,000 homes (mostly flats) were built each year from the mid-1970s to the mid-1980s.[23] And the aim was to create three million new homes through renovation and new-build by 1990.

Although much of the housing built by the GDR has been patronisingly dismissed by Westerners as faceless 'barracks', this is to ignore the innovative technological aspects of the 'Plattenbauten' of the time as well as the spatial and economic context that informed their design. With the acute housing shortage after the war, the priority was to build sufficient housing as rapidly as possible. The Soviet method of using pre-fabricated elements which were easy to put together and build was chosen. But these new housing units were not just thrown up and left abandoned in an urban desert like so many faceless suburban housing projects throughout the Western world.

The government instituted a socio-political planning strategy which prescribed that each new housing complex would include the necessary infrastructure of schools, nurseries, sports facilities, polyclinics, shops and restaurants.

This meant that the new tenants would have everything they need within walking distance and could begin to build good neighbourly relations very quickly. An excellent example of this was the large Halle-Neustadt complex outside the old town of Halle, which was built to house workers employed in the big Buna and Leuna chemical works.

The right to adequate housing has long been enshrined in the UN Charter of Human Rights as a basic human right, yet few countries do more than pay lip service to it. In the GDR it was a reality – everyone had a roof over their head and security of tenure or ownership. Even if that housing was not always of a high standard, particularly in the immediate post-war period of acute housing shortage, it was a space to live, where you could feel secure, with heating and sanitation, as well as affordable, regulated rents.

It cannot be too heavily emphasised what such a right, alongside the right to work, did for people's sense of security and stability, taking a weight off their shoulders and reducing stress.

Voluntary work

Voluntary or honorary work in the GDR played a vital part in the functioning of society, particularly at local or workplace level. There were about 56,000 clubs throughout the GDR catering for a wide variety of interests, from ornithology to philately, archaeology to chess, youth clubs and music classes, all run by unpaid volunteers. Taking on an honorary or voluntary office was seen as social or political work that tapped into that enormous potential reserve to be found in most people. Much work undertaken on behalf of society in the GDR was done by volunteers or honorary participants. And if such work required to be done during normal working hours, then the person concerned would be given time off, with no loss of earnings, to undertake the tasks. Here are a few examples:

Arbeiter- und Bauerninspektion or ABI (Workers and Farmers Inspectorate) was a democratic regulatory body with branches at district and regional level as well as covering a whole industrial sector. It was set up quite early on in the GDR with the express aim of 'fighting and eliminating bureaucracy, rose-tinted reporting, the falsifying of reports, the waste of public property and misuse of public office'. Its members were elected by workers and staff from the various factories and institutions as well as in the trading and services sectors. In towns and villages, there were also People's Inspection Committees (Volkskontrollausschüsse) with a similar function and these were elected from and by local residents.

Most members of these inspection bodies worked on a voluntary basis. The inspectorate arranged for acknowledged specialists and ordinary employees to inspect factories and administrative institutions independently from management. The ABI also inspected, often without any warning, state farms, cultural facilities, health service facilities as well as small trading organisations in the service industry.

The main object of the inspectorate was to spot hazards, secure improvements in working conditions for employees, to identify bottlenecks or even illegal practices and to suggest improvements for management. The conclusions of the inspectorate were discussed in workplace and community residents' meetings.

Volkssolidarität was an association based largely on voluntary support. It was set up in October 1945, in collaboration with political parties, the church, trade unions and women's organisations, to begin with in

Saxony and then expanded throughout the whole territory of the GDR.

It started with promoting solidarity action to ensure elementary survival in the war-devastated country. Later its activities became more focussed on the maintenance of the quality of life for senior citizens and care for those with disabilities.

Solidarity clubs organised a broad range of events and activities: social and cultural events, discussions on topical political issues, popular science lectures, sports, tourism and handicraft circles. Volkssolidarität also helped organise the delivery of meals and home help to needy citizens.

In the 1980s, Volkssolidarität had over two million members and more than 200,000 voluntary workers. These volunteers were motivated largely by the desire to feel they were being socially useful, and were helping to provide a sense of security and comradeship to the elderly and disadvantaged.

Elternaktiv (parents' committee) Every school had parents' committees, comprised of parents of pupils in each form or class, and an additional umbrella committee for the whole school.

A class committee was usually made up of 4-5 parents who would take on the task of supporting the children in the class in attaining their educational goals and serving as a link between the form teacher and the pupils' families. Parents would be given time off work if they were involved in school initiatives like class outings, or sporting and cultural activities and when acting as accompanying adults.

Each parents' committee would agree a work schedule, with deadlines and responsibilities. Tasks would include: monthly discussions with the form teacher with regard to educational achievements of the pupils and to pinpoint where help and support were needed; the organisation of class outings and other events, the planning of topics for after-school activities, organising sporting activities as well as events helping pupils prepare for adult life and choice of career.

Parents might give presentations about their own jobs and professions, and visits might be made to various factories. If acute problems arose in the class, such as a sudden drop in a pupil's work standards or difficulties with fellow pupils, these would be discussed in the parents' committees and possible solutions suggested in collaboration with the form teacher.

Verkehrssicherheitsaktiv or VSA (Traffic Safety Initiative Group) In order to ensure the highest levels of road and traffic safety, a Traffic Safety Initiative Group would be set up within a factory or institution where vehicles were used. Its task was to carry out spot checks on lorries and cars in terms of their safety. It also carried out breathalyser tests on drivers, checked the validity of drivers' licences, and also organised regular traffic and driving instruction courses which were noted in the licence documents of those who had taken part. It gave road safety talks in schools and to local residents groups and organised monthly training courses with a traffic policeman.

These tasks carried out by the VSA contributed considerably to keeping traffic collisions and accidents at low levels.

Such initiatives and organisations helped bring about a more cohesive society, based on solidarity and they also gave people a strong sense of belonging. They felt an integral part of a system in which they were valued as vital contributors to the wellbeing of all.

EDUCATION

A comprehensive system for all age groups

Immediately after the end of the Second World War, East Germany carried out a thorough de-nazification of the teaching staff in schools and other learning institutions. After all, it was these teachers who had been, in the main, willing accomplices in indoctrinating a generation of children with Nazi ideology and the virus of racism. A new generation of teachers was essential if the post-war generation of children was to be freed of this burden. In West Germany, such a thorough clear-out of teaching staffs was never carried out and, in fact, many ex-Nazis were reinstated and even promoted under the 1951 amnesty.

The GDR also carried out a complete re-organisation of the learning process and curricula to overcome decades of privileged access by an elite to education and entrenched class and gender discrimination as well as the old urban-rural divide. This was also essential to rid the educational system of the old racist and supremacist nationalism.

A fully comprehensive school system was introduced with a national curriculum. This meant that school students everywhere studied the same courses and were taught to the same standards. For parents there was no soul-searching about choosing schools – you knew that your local school, whether an inner-city or rural one, would be working to the same standards. The old grammar school (Gymnasium) system, which favoured largely wealthy and middle-class families, giving them a privileged access route to university and the professions, was abolished. There were no private schools – all children went to state schools. At under 30 pupils, classes in both primary and secondary schools were also smaller than in many other countries.

The difference this made to so many working class children in the GDR can be imagined. Jutta Ditfurth, a founding member of the Green Party, describes critically in her autobiography her own experience in the West German school system during the 1960s and how places were being allocated for the local gymnasium (grammar school):

> 'Of course, the daughter of a doctor – after taking the entrance exam – would be allowed to go to the gymnasium,' as would, 'of course, the daughter of an architect. ... But her close friend – a girl from a poorer background – was not offered a place. 'The social status of her mother was too low. She was a worker with no husband.' So her daughter 'lacked the necessary entrance qualifications for higher education.'[24]

Such a divisive educational system was the norm in West Germany, and the teaching, particularly of history, was still very nationalistic and conservative. It was this class privilege and a backward-looking curriculum that the GDR sought to overcome.

The vast majority of children completed ten years of schooling and finished with a certificate of education (equivalent to GCSEs in Britain) to prove that they had completed their basic education and had reached a set standard. Those intending to go on to higher education completed two more years and took their Abitur (A-level equivalent), which was the necessary entrance qualification for college or university. By the end of the 1980s, 95 per cent of all pupils were in schools that would provide them with a completed ten-year school-leaving certificate. A mere five per cent left school after only eight years schooling, but even they would proceed to a technical college for a three-year training, usually in a technical career or in social services and nursing.

If young people did not achieve the academic qualifications they would later need, adult and further education, free of charge, were readily accessible at every stage of their working lives. Thus, young people could continue career training and at the same time study for their A-levels.

The GDR system of continued access to further education was innovative and helped overcome educational discrepancies or personal setbacks. All workers had the opportunity of continuing their education throughout their working lives, and workplaces were obliged to support this. Many industrial and agricultural workers, whose schooling had begun pre-war and who had had no opportunity to study, now had the chance to make up for it. Special 'Worker and Farmer Faculties' were established in the 1950s to provide access courses for those without basic educational qualifications, who wished to go on to higher education. These operated until 1963, when it was considered that they were no longer needed because all generations by then had been fully integrated into the education system.

Since the beginning of the 1960s, a number of specialist schools were created in the GDR in order to offer more intensive support for talented pupils in a number of subjects. These included mathematics and the sciences but also foreign languages, particularly Russian.

Specialisation started at various ages depending on the subject. Specialist language schooling was offered in some primary schools from the age of nine and in special schools from the beginning of secondary education. Maths and sciences admission was, usually, at age 14. All special schools provided additional lessons in the chosen specialities as part of the A-level programme. Not surprisingly, these schools were highly selective. Students had to demonstrate a record of good performance, for example, in the maths olympiad (an annual competition for students, starting at local level and culminating in a national and sometimes international competition). There were also special courses for talented A-level students at some universities.

Music was particularly fostered, and those with talent were given the opportunity of learning to play an instrument at a special music school. There were about 100 special schools for music as well as about 300 extramural sites. That meant that, in the 1980s, more than 36,000 young people could have extra curricular lessons in playing an instrument, singing and dancing. About 300 students per year went on to study music as their main subject. There were also special music schools for particularly talented children who were able to attend from six years of age, i.e. the beginning of formal schooling. Again, here music was the specialism in addition to the normal national curriculum.

The other area of specialism was sport. Already from the 1950s onwards, there were a number of specialist sports schools and by 1989, there were 25 of these with more than 10,000 pupils. It was in these schools that the foundation for the impressive sports achievements of the GDR were laid.

School books were either free or heavily subsidised and available at affordable prices. In an attempt to redress the decades of discrimination towards working class and farm workers' children, a form of positive discrimination was introduced for university entrance to overcome this (comparable, perhaps, with the attempt in the USA to actively promote blacks).

In order to provide children and young people with a broad spectrum of developmental opportunity and to stimulate extra-curricular interests, schools offered involvement in an increasing number of activity groups

(AGs) that took place after the normal school day. In the GDR, the formal school day finished around midday, leaving time in the afternoons for extra-curricular activities. Almost all pupils took part in such activities, some took part in several; teachers, would lead these activities alongside parents and local residents. Work as a leader of such an activity group was considered as voluntary and seen as a contribution to society. Such groups could include orchestras, young naturalists groups, vehicle maintenance, amateur radio, model building, hand ball, gymnastics, sewing, chemistry for young people, photography circles, athletics, football, brass bands, beekeeping, drawing, history studies, choirs, philately, sailing, chess, first aid and school garden work.

All university students were awarded grants, which were minimal but enough to survive on, especially since student accommodation was heavily subsidised (a room in a student hostel cost the equivalent of about £3 a month). Students could obtain additional grants if they achieved good end-of-year results. This was a stimulus for students to take their studies seriously.

Apprentices also received payments and, since the early 1980s, even A-level students received a small maintenance allowance to give them more independence.

The egalitarianism of the school system meant that children from all different backgrounds mixed and made friends; there were no feelings of class difference, of material deprivation or of exclusion. This led to a much more relaxed and happier society, devoid of the tensions that can be caused by class and large wealth differentials as in western societies.

Despite the fact that the educational system in the GDR was widely praised and recognised as one of the best in the world, after unification it was abolished, and the discriminatory three-tier secondary school system of the Federal Republic imposed – with consequences for those children who now found themselves streamed off into different types of school at a young age.

As an interesting anecdote, when, some years after unification, a delegation of German educationists visited Finland to observe teaching methods there – as it is widely recognised as having one of the best and most successful educational systems in the world – the Finns thought it rather odd that the Germans should be coming to them, saying that Finland had garnered many of its ideas from the GDR educational system.

The polytechnical principle

One of the chief innovations of the GDR school system was 'polytechnical' education. This completely new approach to education was introduced in 1958 together with a comprehensive school system. It was an attempt to better integrate schools into the social fabric and the world of work. It was also intended to overcome the lop-sided view of education as only 'brain-work'. This idea went back to discussions held in the working class movement during the 19th century and the theories of progressive pedagogues in the Weimar Republic who had emphasised the need for a link between education and material production.

Already in the nurseries, children were able to learn about the world of work: e.g. they were encouraged to observe the work of the cooks or the caretakers and to appreciate how much effort is involved in such essential work. Six to ten-year-olds took part in gardening programmes in their school gardens, learning how to sow seeds, handle various gardening tools and to appreciate the work involved in growing things. Once a week, six to twelve-year-olds had handicraft lessons (Werkunterricht) where they worked, dependent on age, with paper, cardboard, wood and plastic as well as with modular construction systems. At the age of

13, polytechnic lessons started and were realised (and paid for) in more than 5,000 enterprises. All schools participated, including special schools and A-level classes. One day per week pupils undertook a day of practical work in one of the participating firms in their locality.

The emphasis was on production techniques, machine engineering, electronics and the automation of the production process. In addition, pupils had courses in technical drawing. In special workshops, separated from production in the respective enterprise, 13 and 14-year-olds would be given instruction in metalworking, while 15 and 16-year-olds participated more directly in the production process giving them the opportunity of learning about the various processes; 17 and 18 year olds worked as part of larger teams during periods of work experience.

This system not only gave young people a true sense of what working life was all about, but showed them how the necessities of life are produced and, meeting and working alongside manual workers, they developed a respect for them and the contribution they make to society. This kind of education placed emphasis on a broad general knowledge, including mathematics, science, economics and the arts as well as the essential element of linking theory with practice, i.e. links were developed between school and the world of work. It also forged stronger social links between schools and workplaces, between workers and students as well as teachers, which were often extended into the social and cultural spheres. This system was only possible because all larger companies were state-owned and even farms were either co-operatives or state-owned, so they were obliged to co-operate in making the process work.

The successful introduction of polytechnical education as a stand-alone subject that included theoretical principles, economic implications, as well as the practical teaching of manual work was unique to the GDR educational system.

It was actually much admired among a number of pedagogues in the West, but never introduced there – and since unification it has been abolished in that form, although secondary school students do have to complete three-weeks of work experience in a business or factory at age 14.

ECONOMY

Workers' rights

It was not merely in the rhetoric that workers and workers' rights were placed high on the policy agendas of the socialist countries. After all, the main aim of any socialist state, based on the theories of Marx and Engels, was to achieve the freedom of workers from exploitation and oppression; they were seen as the motor and central pillar of society. Work itself was elevated to a place of pride and esteem and, even if you were in a lower paid job, you were valued for the work you did as a necessary contribution to the functioning of society. The socialist countries were also designated 'workers' states and it was not merely an empty phrase when the GDR government argued that the workers, who produced the commodities that society needed, should be placed at the forefront of society. Those who did heavy manual work, like miners or steel workers, enjoyed certain privileges: better wages and additional health care than those in less strenuous or dangerous professions.

The GDR had one of the most comprehensive workers' rights legislation of any country in the world. From 1950 onwards, there was a guaranteed right to work. This right applied to everybody, including disabled people and those with criminal records. Employers were made responsible for the training and integration of everyone. This meant that everybody felt they had a place in society and were needed. This was particularly important for disabled people and those who wanted a new start in life after being convicted of a crime.

Working people were under a much more relaxed discipline in the workplace. Because there was job security and it was almost impossible to be sacked, an authoritarian discipline was difficult, if not impossible, to impose. In Western countries work discipline is invariably enforced by the implicit threat of job loss.

In the GDR, only in cases of serious misconduct or incompetence would employees be sacked. There were individual cases where employees were sacked illegally for what was considered 'oppositional' or 'anti-state behaviour', but usually the sanction would involve demotion or being transferred to a different workplace. This job security gave employees a sense of confidence and a considerable power in the workplace. It meant that workers could and would voice criticism over inefficiencies or bad management without having to fear for their job. Job security and lack of fear about losing one's job was probably one of the greatest advantages the socialist system offered working people. Even in cases where a worker was sacked from one job, other alternative work would be offered, even if not on the same level. The other side of the coin was that there was also a social obligation to work – the GDR had no system of unemployment benefit, because the concept of unemployment did not exist.

Workplace grievances did of course occur and sometimes they were not solved to the satisfaction of the workforce. Occasionally, in such situations, work stoppages would take place. In 1971, for instance, 48 wildcat strikes took place and 14 in 1981.[25] Strikes were not officially banned, but were certainly not encouraged and every effort was made to solve problems before they reached such a stage.

Workers were involved in discussions of workplace issues and the organisation of the work process. It is true though, that real involvement in the economic and production plans of their workplaces fell short of the optimum, and consultation often became a formal procedure rather than a creative and genuinely democratic process.

The national trade union (FDGB) in the GDR was often dismissed in the West as merely a state-run organisation to prevent workers rebelling or going on strike. However, even though it did not have the independence from the state that trade unions have in the West, it played a key role in ensuring the health and safety and wellbeing of the workforce. It was responsible for ensuring the delivery of basic social services, which were paid for by social insurance contributions. This had been a traditional demand of the trade union movement in Germany.

According to GDR labour law, there was a general duty on the part of employers to provide social care for their workforces. That meant for large employers (e.g. factories, local authorities and universities) an obligation to ensure the provision of healthcare, childcare, work canteens, sports facilities, housing and even holiday places for adults and children.

Every factory and other large employers had a medical centre on their premises, usually including several specialists as well as dental care, providing primary medical care for the workforce. This meant that seeing a doctor was easy, illnesses could be diagnosed early and expert advice was at hand. One consequence of this prophylactic system was that occupational illness decreased and early diagnosis prevented potential complications in the case of illness.

Employers also supported employees with obtaining housing, as this was, for most of the GDR's existence in short supply. Enterprises would be allocated a certain number of flats by local councils. Local enterprises would often be given priority in terms of allocation of housing to new employees. This meant that there would be less stress for the new employee and flat hunting would be less problematic in a new town. Housing commissions, with input from trade unions, were responsible for developing plans for flat allocation to the workforce in accordance with certain basic criteria.

Employers provided crèches and kindergartens for the children of their employees. These, like the nurseries in the communities, were free of charge apart from a small contribution towards food. Often an employee could choose whether to take up an offer from the workplace nursery or find one nearer home if more convenient.

It was standard to have canteens in the workplace. Since the midday meal is the main meal for Germans, it was particularly important to have a choice of nutritious meals and these were, like most basic foodstuffs, subsidised.

Employers, together with the trade unions, supported the creation of recreational facilities for employees. Hundreds of factories had their own holiday homes which employees were able to use at a fraction of the real costs. The trade unions, too, built hotel-like holiday homes that were subsidised so that a holiday for a family, usually only paying 25 per cent of the actual cost, became affordable. By the 1980s, around 80 per cent of the population was able to go on some form of annual holiday, although most of these would be taken in the GDR itself, many in one of such centres at very low prices.[26]

In addition, employers, together with the trade unions, organised holiday provision for the children of their workforce. These camps, where holidays were usually about three weeks, were available to all children up to the age of 14. Already in 1951, almost 240,000 children had been to such holiday camps and in 1988, about 1.3 million children spent part of their holidays in these summer camps that were virtually free. Their existence meant that the six-week school summer holidays did not become a problem for (working) parents. They could be sure that their children would be supervised by properly trained staff and that they would have an enjoyable time.

Factories and other large employers tended to have a

range of sports facilities, including gyms, swimming pools and sports fields, which were available to staff free of charge. After-work sports activities were encouraged and supported, and many employers had their own teams and sports groups.

Another area of social responsibility was in the legal field. All large employers had what were called 'Conflict Commissions' – lay courts staffed by employees. The aim was, wherever possible, to offer re-education to those who had done wrong, rather than punish them. In 1988, there were more than 250,000 citizens involved in the running of Conflict Commissions. Similar commissions also existed in the communities where they were responsible for dealing with minor crimes and disputes between neighbours. Again, the emphasis was on mediation rather than punishment.

It was realised early on that many small conflicts and straightforward legal issues could be dealt with on a local level, often without the need for professional judicial input or going to court. Conflict Commissions were already in existence from 1953 onwards, and represented an enormous and innovative breakthrough. They were made up of one's own peers from the workplace or residential area. The Commissions could not make custodial sentences, nor would they sit on cases of serious crimes, like murder or treason. Most decisions would involve proposals for rehabilitation, therapy and recompense for victims. They helped overcome potentially unnecessary judicial log-jams in the courts, were far less intimidating for those brought before them and solved many problems without recourse to more draconian measures.

Employees in factories or working for other big employers usually worked in teams (Brigaden). These teams were the centre not just of work but social interaction. According to a basic concept of socialist practice, everyone was to be given the opportunity for their all-round personal development. With this in mind, a broad range of activities outside work was encouraged and supported by the employer. Thus teams as a group would visit the theatre or an art exhibition, go on outings and bowling nights, do voluntary work and maintain contacts with local schools where mentoring teams (Patenbrigaden) would develop close and collaborative relationships and visit the schools regularly. It was these joint activities that made for a special atmosphere in the workplace. Work was not just a means of earning a living but a place for social inter-action and the basis for friendship and community spirit.

Productivity in the GDR was lower than in similar industrialised nations in the West. This was in no small measure due to its policy of full employment, which meant that there were often comparably more workers and staff in the workplaces than in the West. And the social provisions described above added to the overall cost. Working conditions were, generally, less stressful and there was a more relaxed atmosphere in the absence of the draconian time-and-motion pressures so well established in the West. In this sense, the GDR was more oriented towards a future in which the workplace would be a place where citizens could find fulfilment and a sense of social purpose, not what it has so often become in the West, a place of stress and intense exploitation. Workers and management did not feel they were in a permanent marketplace where they had to sell themselves; they had the time and space to be able to reflect on work processes and the work situation in a more fundamental and long-term way.

To illustrate the contrast between working conditions in East and West, perhaps the following can serve as an example: The television electronics company VEB Fernsehelektronik was based in Treptow, East Berlin. In 1983, it was modernised with the help of Japanese expertise in order to produce colour television tubes. The assembly line speeds, though, were based on the East European model rather than the Asian one. After the collapse of the GDR, the company was bought by the South Korean company Samsung. 'Now, whenever the door closes behind me I'm in Asia,' one of the workers says. 'Senior management has been replaced by Koreans. Without installing new machinery the tempo of the assembly line has been doubled. Employees now work a three-shift system, round the clock, and the stress is considerable. No rest breaks are allowed, but permanent overtime and weekend special shifts are demanded by management, for just a little extra in one's pocket. Health and safety is neglected and there were several serious accidents soon after the Koreans took over'. This man's girlfriend, he relates, received 'a large electric shock while working, and her whole body was shaking and she became ice-cold and her face was as white as chalk. The foreman maintained that it was only a discharge of harmless static electricity and she was allowed to rest for a whole ten minutes, before having to return to work.' That is an example of capitalism in the raw and if, as a worker, you don't like it there will be enough agency or migrant workers queuing up to take your job. This is what has happened to many factories and workplaces in East Germany since unification.[27]

Working people in the GDR, in the main, revealed a level of self-confidence, and feeling of self-worth and dignity that is often missing among the workforces in capitalist countries. This influenced the mental health of individual workers and helped cement a social cohesion – positive impacts that cannot be underestimated. In the GDR, burn-out in the workplace was rare and no one had to worry about unemployment.

Pros and cons of central planning

Lacking the industrial base and the massive Marshall Plan aid that West Germany received after the end of the war, East Germany would have remained underdeveloped.

Without a planned economy, central state guidance and a concentration of economic forces on particular focal points, it would not have been possible to get the country back on its feet again. The first and second five-year plans managed to establish the first heavy and chemical as well as energy supply industries.

The creation of a merchant marine port in Rostock, new shipyards, a gas production plant, the building of an iron foundry complex in a new town built for that purpose from scratch, a new oil refinery and the steady industrialisation of the northern regions all bore witness to the success of this policy. According to Peter Grabley, a former member of the GDR's State Planning Commission, the real German economic miracle took place in the 'little GDR', and this is hardly an exaggeration, given what was achieved in only 40 years.[28]

The GDR – a country with only 16 million people – became a developed industrialised nation that was virtually self-sufficient. In industry alone, three million people were employed, almost a million of those in the machine tool sector. In addition, there were precision engineering, shipbuilding, chemical and electrical engineering sectors, to name just the largest ones. On the world market, the GDR was recognised as a leading industrial nation (the name Carl Zeiss Jena was world renowned) and, above all, it was an exporting nation for machinery and tool-making equipment, printing presses, furniture and musical instruments, like the renowned Blüthner piano. By 1988, it was exporting 39 per cent of its total industrial output; most of this (69 per cent) went to Eastern Europe but a not insignificant amount to western countries.[29]

Its economy was one of the most successful and most stable of the socialist bloc and, according to UN figures, the GDR was among the leading 20 industrialised countries of the world.[30] The economy was largely characterised by the public ownership of key industries and institutions and by a central planning and regulation process. Over 90 per cent of all assets in the GDR were owned by the people in the form of 'publicly-owned enterprises' (VEBs). At the time of unification, there were 12,354 such enterprises.[31] There were also semi-private enterprises in which the state took a share by investing, often 50 per cent or more of the capital. And there was a small but, in terms of output, quite significant private sector. According to GDR statistics, in 1985, there were about 176,800 private entrepreneurs who were responsible for 2.8 per cent of GDP.

The private sector included craftsmen, wholesalers and retailers, farmers and gardeners as well as those who worked freelance, like artists, writers or photographers. People working in crafts and trades sometimes operated as individual undertakings or as members of co-operatives (PGHs). Private companies in the GDR were invariably small, and few employed more than ten people. Trade cooperatives were often larger enterprises: retail supermarkets, house-builders, service undertakings and agricultural units. It was thus a mixed economy but with the overwhelming majority of companies being owned and run by the state on behalf of the people.

Profits made by the publicly-owned enterprises were to a large extent centralised to be distributed according to the needs of society as a whole; but a large proportion was reinvested to support the further development of the economy. That was of particular importance during the first ten years of the GDR's existence.

In the 1960s, many individual enterprises operating in similar fields were brought together to form linked units (VVBs), which worked closely together in terms of technical co-operation, research and development and took overall responsibility for their own sector. This meant that central planning was also complemented by a certain decentralisation. The central planning authorities would set overall production goals, but each VVB would determine its own internal financing, use of technology and the allocation of resources. In the 1970s, state combines (Kombinate) were created in order to forge even more efficient economic units. These were large conglomerates created in the different manufacturing sectors with tens of thousands of employees.

The directors of these combines (equivalent to a CEO in the West) came, almost exclusively, from working-class backgrounds. They all learned a trade and later gained higher education qualifications both in their trade and in the field of economics. Because of this background, they had a more empathetic relationship with the employees working in their combine. They did not just see the workforce as a means of fulfilling the plan. For them the social side of employment was important too, as were health and safety and wellbeing. The rationale was to demonstrate to employees that they were valued and thus motivate them to contribute their best. It is interesting that the majority of these managing directors emphasise today, after experiencing a different economic system, the importance of social support for an overall climate of satisfaction in an enterprise. They say that an enterprise that makes billions in profit could easily afford the additional costs of providing decent working and living conditions for its workforce.[32]

The centrally-planned economy meant enterprises were guided by a whole series of indicators (productivity, profit, labour availability, investment, wage funds, export etc.). If plans were fulfilled, then bonuses were paid, and these were an important stimulus for the enterprises themselves and for individual employees.

Innovation groups and competition between brigades were also important means of promoting increases in production. The director of each enterprise was also obliged to organise discussions on planning with the trade unions and employees. Employees, too, could put forward proposals and suggestions on the best ways of realising the plans. But these discussions which were a good idea in principle were often only carried out as a formality.

The GDR's economic system enabled the government to plan growth, set priorities and determine vital areas for investment and expansion; but there was also the downside that centralised planning on such a scale could be cumbersome. While having a distinct advantage in terms of national goals, distribution and allocation of resources, it also had a negative impact: once the national economic plan had been accepted its implementation took on an inflexible logic and if unforeseen shortages or unexpected rises in raw material prices occurred, there was little or no leeway to rectify things.

The underlying principle of the GDR's social model was based on the Soviet one which accepted the leading role of the Party taking key decisions even on the economy. This was based on the assumption of Party infallibility in the face of specialist advice. As a result, the economy was subservient to political priorities or, in other words, was determined by groups or individuals in the Party leadership.[33] This involved decisions on which products to manufacture or not – very much based on overall Comecon (Council for Mutual Economic Assistance) planning – and where investments would be channeled. According to the long-term head of the GDR state planning commission, it was this dogma of politics over economic decision-making that led to sometimes intractable difficulties in the economy.[34]

However, there was one vital factor that held back the GDR economy (and that of other socialist countries) and that was a strict boycott by Western governments, banning the export of technology to the socialist world. This placed considerable burdens on the GDR's economic development. The Coordinating Committee on Multilateral Export Controls (CoCom) was set up by the Western allies in 1949 under pressure from the USA in order to prevent the Soviet

Union and its allies obtaining western technology and expertise. Its aims were to draw up lists of banned exports, organise consultations on the updating of latest technologies and meetings to monitor the efficacy of the trade restrictions. This boycott also meant that the GDR had to develop many products from scratch and at great cost although they were already being traded on the world's markets. This had a negative impact on the development and availability of many consumer products.

That western embargo on the export of technology to the Eastern Bloc meant that the GDR had to produce much of what it needed itself, often at considerable cost. As an example, a director of a combine in the GDR recalls, 'Our combine brought together the total production of rotating electrical motors, from the smallest for a camera or a tape recorder mechanism, to large machines of several megawatts. The annual production was, towards the end of the eighties around 12 million electrical units, in an astounding 100,000 variations'.[27]

It is not easy to make a conclusive statistical comparison between the GDR economy and those of the capitalist countries because the basis on which statistics were collected in the socialist countries and the methods of financial accounting were often very different from those in the West. However, the GDR's ranking as one of the world's leading industrial nations and second amongst the Comecon countries was widely accepted.

Although the GDR's economy was a success, compared with most other medium-sized countries, it did suffer from acute shortages and log-jams in a number of areas. By the late 1980s, the income of the population had grown, partly due to the consistently low (subsidised) prices for everyday goods, and there was an increasing demand for higher value consumer products that were either scarce or not at all available. This led to growing dissatisfaction and criticism.

Farming and Co-operatives

After the victory of the Red Army and its occupation of the eastern third of Germany, large landowners, mainly the 'Junker' class (the landed aristocracy that had traditionally been a pillar of support for German militarism), were expropriated and the land distributed to landless peasants and small farmers. In September 1947, the Soviet military administration announced the completion of agrarian reform throughout the Soviet zone. The report listed 12,355 estates, which had been seized and redistributed to 119,000 landless farmers, 83,000 refugee families, and some 300,000 agricultural labourers.

But many new farmers soon found that the acreage of the individual pieces of land given to them through the land reform was not large enough to provide a decent living; and often the new farmers did not possess the expertise or the machinery to work the land efficiently. The government therefore supported the idea of co-operatives. It was felt that they would help ensure a full and efficient use of machinery and guarantee higher agricultural production. A vital support for the newly established co-operatives were the so-called Machine and Tractor Stations (MTS) where big and expensive machinery could be hired out. This avoided the need for each co-operative to buy its own machinery. Later this agricultural machinery was handed over to the co-ops.

A significant feature of the co-ops was the fact that all members had equal rights and their democratic participation was not dependent on how much land each brought into the co-op, nor on their gender or age. Each co-op had its own constitution. There were different types of co-operatives with different levels of common ownership. In type 1 co-ops, only land was brought into the unit, while animal husbandry was still carried out privately. In type 2, in addition to the land, those animals that were needed to work the land, as well as machinery, became part of the co-op. In type 3 co-ops, everything needed for agricultural production became part of the co-op. In all three types the land remained the titular property of the farmers who joined the co-op. Even in type 3 co-ops, the farmers were able to retain one acre of land for growing their own fruit and vegetables and were able to raise their own animals for private use or for the market.

Farmers in co-ops had no fixed salaries; their income depended on the productivity of the co-op. Co-ops usually had contracts with various food-processing factories, which took around two thirds of their overall production. The rest was paid out in kind to the members in addition to normal salaries paid on the basis of individual performance. In addition, farmers received top-up payments relating to the size of the land each had contributed to the co-op. However, it was soon recognised that this system of payment would only serve to perpetuate a situation of inequality. It was therefore adjusted later so that everyone would receive the same average payment.

Co-ops as such paid no tax; instead, surplus money was paid into a special fund for the purchase of machinery, maintenance, transport and seed. There was also a fund for assisting members in emergencies, and one for the organisation of cultural projects and for bonuses. At the end of the year, a bonus was paid based on the overall profitability of the co-op. This was always a welcome addition to basic earnings.

In the 1970s, all co-ops were transformed into type 3 undertakings and they started working together on a regional basis. On the insistence of the SED, these larger co-operative groups then started to specialise in either arable farming or livestock production, increasingly on an industrial scale. This was a development that many farmers found quite controversial because it meant, amongst other things, increased transportation and administrative responsibility and therefore expense. It was later partially reversed.

One of the big advantages of agricultural co-ops was that individual farmers and labourers had, for the first time, a fixed working day, guaranteed holidays and the possibility of retirement without the worry of what would happen to the farm.

The co-ops would organise the cultural life in the village, support its members in building homes and in gaining qualifications. It also provided childcare and holiday places. All this contributed towards the aim, anchored in the GDR constitution, of equalising living conditions in towns and villages. Often a number of villages would form a co-operate union, as this made it possible to jointly set up cultural premises, restaurants, shops, as well as medical services that would involve too much outlay for one village alone.[36]

The improvement of education was another direct result of forming co-ops. Farm workers were provided with the opportunity of obtaining relevant qualifications. Special access courses were introduced to prepare them for technical colleges or universities. For women, special women-only courses were also arranged in order to support female farm workers in gaining qualifications. For many this would have been the first time they had the chance of obtaining a qualification in their field of work.

Through the co-ops the number of people with qualifications increased considerably: in 1963, 18 per cent of men and only 8.5 per cent of women had a relevant qualification; by 1989, the numbers had increased to 94 per cent (men) and 92 per cent (women). Larger villages had walk-in clinics with several specialist doctors. Nurseries, especially at harvest time, were particularly useful as were after-school clubs. Bus services and their frequency were increased in order to make it possible for people in outlying villages to reach their nearest town by public transport.

Despite some early opposition to giving up their individual land-holdings, most farmers came to see the sense of co-operatives and enjoyed the fruits of their success. They became one of the big achievements of the GDR, proving to be efficient and better for the workforce. For the first time in history, agricultural workers were freed from round-the-clock, year-in, year-out work just to make a living. With agricultural co-operatives run on an industrial scale, agricultural workers enjoyed fixed-hours working and shift systems, had regular holidays, childcare, training opportunities, and workplace canteens. All this helped stem the flight from the countryside to the towns (as has happened in many other countries). During the lifetime of the GDR the percentage of citizens living in the cities with over 100,000 inhabitants barely rose. The increasing use of technology and modern techniques on the farms also made the work more attractive to young people and helped retain them in the countryside. It is significant that the number of members in the co-ops increased over time because young people became members, no longer leaving at the first opportunity for the towns (in the 1980s, membership of co-ops increased by more than 10 per cent).[37]

It was also a fact that the per capita production figures of most co-operatives were better than those of individual farmers in the West. The co-operative principle, particularly in the agricultural sphere, demonstrated that it could offer a third way between the often barely economically viable family farms and industrialised farming, which has been responsible for the destruction of social structures and the rural environment in many countries.

After unification, when the whole economy was privatised at break-neck speed, the co-operatives came under enormous pressure. However, the main reason they could challenge the threatened expropriation was that the farm workers and not the state owned the land. This meant it could not legally be taken away from them and they could make their own decisions as to what to do with it. Because of their positive experience working in the co-operatives, the vast majority of farmers did not want a return to individual farming. However, the co-ops had to battle against discrimination anchored in Federal German law that favoured individual over collective ownership. In addition, they suddenly faced imposed fictitious debts that were near impossible to pay in the changed economic circumstances. As a result, many co-operatives were forced to give up. Today only a few survive and about 80 per cent of the jobs in agriculture have been lost.[38]

Public transport

A publicly-owned transport system meant that national timetables for all rail and bus services could be developed, that were fully coordinated with each other. All public transport was highly subsidised making it affordable for everyone. There was a strong emphasis on it, not only for ideological reasons, but because there was a shortage of private cars. Car production had been deliberately under-prioritised, which meant that people had to wait for years in order to buy a car. This waiting list also meant that those cars already on the road were given a much longer life than those in the West and almost everyone became an expert in car repair and renovation – skills now highly sought after by those who resent the wastage in the new throwaway society.

The GDR's Trabant car has been the subject of much ridicule and became symbolic for the country's car industry. It is little known though that the other major GDR car, the much bigger Wartburg, was actually exported to the West, including the UK, during the 1970s.

Since the oil crisis of the early 1970s, there was great emphasis placed on shifting freight onto rail. There was a huge investment in containerisation and the building of new dedicated terminals for container transport. This meant that by the end of the 1980s, the transport of goods by rail had risen sevenfold and transportation by road was thus reduced. In order to avoid empty loads, a central office coordinated all long-distance transport.

With unification, this container system was all but destroyed because in a privatised economy there was no demand for a nationally coordinated transportation system. In the GDR, 77 per cent of all goods were transported by rail, whereas in the new Germany only 18 per cent are.

HEALTH SERVICE

Anchored in the constitution of the GDR was the right to healthcare. In this respect, the system was not dissimilar to the one in Britain. It was free at the point of use, and this included dentistry and ophthalmology. All medication on prescription was also free. Victorian-style wards in hospitals were unknown; even older hospitals had smaller wards than in Britain and were not open-plan, each having its own door. In the 1970s, modern hospitals were built with rooms for no more then two or three patients.

What was different in the GDR health service was its basic approach. Emphasis was placed on prevention rather than later cure and also on interdisciplinary collaboration. Outpatient treatment involved a much broader conceptual approach than in Britain. By employing a combination of preventative, diagnostic and therapeutic resources linked with rehabilitation and social care, hospital treatment could, in many cases, be avoided. This approach was based in the so-called polyclinic and walk-in clinic system.

A polyclinic was not just run by general practitioners as health centres are in Britain. They would have at least six specialist departments, an X-ray unit, laboratories and a pharmacy. In terms of staff, they would have between 20-40 doctors and up to 200 other employees, e.g. nurses, laboratory technicians and administrative staff. Walk-in centres were slightly smaller but also had a multi-disciplinary approach with a combination of general practitioners and specialists. The advantage for patients was that they could often be treated directly in the polyclinic without the need of having to go to a hospital with the inevitable delays of transfer procedures. Polyclinics had another advantage, both for those using them and those working there: they had extended opening hours (made possible by a shift system and the relatively large number of staff employed). Because of the shift system, doctors as well as other staff had normal eight-hour working days (rather than the 10-12 hours typical for individual practices).

In rural areas, villages would be linked with a polyclinic in the nearest town. A community nurse (Gemeindeschwester) was responsible for care of the people living in the village. The community nurse system was a unique concept developed by the GDR. It was not the same as the British district nurse. A community nurse worked independently in a village. She (it was usually a 'she') had very close contact and was therefore familiar with the people in her locality. When someone fell ill or there was an emergency it was she who would make the initial diagnosis, help with basic treatment and contact a doctor or hospital if needed. Once a week a doctor from the polyclinic would hold a surgery in each village. Community nurses received a comprehensive training, which was ongoing even after they were fully qualified. All 5,500 of these special nurses lost their jobs on unification because the West German system, with its emphasis on individual private medical practices, was unable to accommodate them. They had a choice of staying on and working in a much narrower field, like geriatric care, or they had to leave. There is, unsurprisingly perhaps, now an increasing shortage of comprehensive health care in rural areas because few doctors wish to move there.

Once a week a paediatrician from the polyclinic would visit local nurseries in order to check the health of the children and to administer necessary vaccinations. This helped in the monitoring of the health of the children and it helped working parents avoid obligatory visits to the doctor for check-ups. Polyclinics were also linked with local primary schools where regular screenings and dental checks were made. This helped to identify early any potential health problems or domestic neglect. The emphasis in healthcare was clearly placed on prevention rather than treatment, which is, in the long run, much more cost effective and advantageous for everyone. The importance of polyclinics becomes clear from the fact that 50 per cent of all doctors in the GDR worked in them.

After unification, almost all the polyclinics and walk-in clinics were closed within two years and medical care is now provided by individual private medical practices, paid for through a nationwide insurance system in accordance with the system prevalent in the FRG.

Although not specific to the GDR, or the socialist countries as a whole, there was also an excellent sanatorium system which provided long periods of recuperation or rehabilitation in spa resorts or retreats in the countryside (often in former stately homes), for those deemed to be in need of such care. This was particularly valuable for those suffering chronic illness or in need of recuperative care impossible to find at home. What was special in the GDR was that single mothers in need of respite care were given the opportunity to recuperate in mother and child sanatoria free of charge.

CULTURE, MEDIA AND SPORT

Culture

During the forty years of its existence, a unique GDR culture developed in the country and it differed substantially from that in the West. Its main differentiating characteristic was the widespread involvement and participation of ordinary people not just as consumers of culture, but as active participants in creative activity. In the arts, a resonance was engendered by the ongoing tension between demands by artists for more freedom of expression, on the one hand, and strictures imposed by the party and state on the other.

Many artists attempted to create a genuine socialist realist art form, but one which at the same time pushed the boundaries of that form. In theatre it built on the iconoclasm of Brecht and Piscator's epic principles as well as Soviet agit-prop, in painting it had its roots in the stark realism of artists like Käthe Kollwitz, Otto Dix and Ernst Barlach, and in literature through the writing of authors like Lion Feuchtwanger, Anna Seghers, Stefan Hermlin and Stefan Heym.

Since the early days of the Soviet Union, the Bolsheviks and later communist parties everywhere placed a great emphasis on culture and on the contribution cultural workers could make to the building of socialism. One of the first things the Soviet Army of occupation did at the end of the war, was attempt to resuscitate cultural activity in a war-ravaged and demoralised Germany.

The one thing the Russians could never get their head around was how a country with such a high level of culture, a nation that had produced a Bach and a Beethoven, a Goethe and a Schiller could have carried out such barbaric crimes in other countries. The Soviet army had cultural officers attached to each battalion and the war had hardly ended before they began seeking out cultural workers and encouraging them to take up their batons, musical instruments, pens and paintbrushes again. Temporary cinemas were established, orchestras formed, theatres opened and publishing houses set up.

In contrast to West Germany, in the Soviet Zone and later in the GDR, there was also an early emphasis on making films about the Nazi period as a means of educating and informing a nation ignorant of or in denial about what had happened.

The first anti-Nazi and anti-war film to be made in the whole of Germany was *Die Mörder sind unter uns* (Murderers among us, 1946) directed by the West Berlin-based Wolfgang Staudte with full Soviet support. Among later anti-Nazi films made in the GDR were: *Rat der Götter* (Council of the Gods, 1950) about the production of poison gas by IG Farben for the concentration camps, *Nackt unter Wölfen* (Naked amongst Wolves, 1963), based on a true story about a small Jewish boy who was hidden in a concentration camp and thus saved. *Werner Holt* (1965) – about the life of young men in Hitler's army, *Gefrorene Blitze* (Frozen Flashes, 1967) – about the development of the V2 rocket by the Nazis; *Ich war Neunzehn* (I was Nineteen, 1968) – the true story of a young German who returns to Germany in the uniform of a Red Army soldier with the victorious Russian troops. Almost two decades passed before West Germany attempted to confront the war and its Nazi past. And the film *Das Boot* (1981) is more about the heroics of German U-boat crews than about understanding Nazi ideology. *Das schreckliche Maedchen* (Nasty Girl, 1990) was a rare exception, as was *Downfall* (2004), a film about Hitler's last days.

The GDR had more theatres per capita than any other country in the world and in no other country were there more orchestras in relation to population size or territory. With 90 professional orchestras, GDR citizens had three times more opportunity of accessing live music, than those in the FRG, 7.5 times more than in the USA and 30 times more than in the UK. It also had one of the world's highest book publishing figures. This small country with its very limited economic resources, even in the fifties was spending double the amount per head on cultural activities than the FRG.[39]

Every town of 30,000 or more inhabitants in the GDR had its theatre and cinema as well as other cultural venues. It had roughly half as many theatres as the Federal Republic, despite having less than a third of the population (178 compared with 346 in the FRG).

Subsidised tickets to the theatre and concerts were always priced so that everyone could afford to go. Many factories and institutions had regular block-bookings for their workers which were avidly taken up. School pupils from the age of 14 were also encouraged to go to the theatre once a month and schools were able to obtain tickets at vastly reduced prices. All the theatres had permanent ensembles of actors who received a regular salary. Plays and operas were performed on a repertory basis, providing everyone in the ensemble with a variety of roles.

All towns and even many villages had their own 'Houses of Culture', owned by the local communities and open for all to use. These were places that offered performance venues, workshop space and facilities for celebratory gatherings, discos, drama groups etc. There was a lively culture of local music and folk-song groups, as well as classical musical performance.

Very different to the situation in West Germany, was the widespread establishment in the GDR of workers' cultural groups – from literary circles, artists groups to ceramic and photography workshops. These were actively encouraged and financially supported by the state, local authorities or the workplace. Discussions of books and literature, often together with authors, were a regular occurrence, even in the remotest of villages.

The 'Kulturbund' (Cultural Association) was a national organisation of over one million members that organised a wide range of cultural events around the country, from concerts, lectures on a wide variety of subjects to art appreciation classes. To begin with it was set up, in 1945, as a movement to bring together interested intellectuals and artists, on the basis of an anti-fascist and humanist outlook, with the aim of promoting a 'national re-birth' and 'of regaining the trust and respect of the world'. From 1949 onwards many smaller cultural groups joined the national Cultural Association. Soon, 'commissions' and 'working groups' for specific areas were established: educational, musical, architectural and craft groups, followed by photographic, press, philatelic, fine arts groups and others. The Association also had its own monthly journal and weekly newspaper.

The art form 'Socialist Realism' has always been decried and ridiculed in the West, caricatured in the constantly circulated images of monumental statues of muscle-bound male workers and buxom, peasant women in heroic poses. However, such a view ignores those many realist artists who were not 'court-appointed' or monumentalists but who chose a realist mode of expression freely.

Many artists in the communist countries simply preferred to place human beings and social reality at the centre of their art, as did most muralists and many painters in the West. It should not be dismissed out of hand. Many continued the strong realist tradition, taking it forward into new realms. It also connected with ordinary people who saw themselves, their lives and their questions and criticisms taken up by artists. While some conformed and became state-sponsored artists, churning out often mediocre art, many others ploughed their own furrow and their work aroused avid interest among the people. This could be seen not only in painting and sculpture but graphics, the theatre, music, literature and, though less so, also in the cinema.

A number of artists did reject the unnecessary ideological fetters as well as banal socialist realist platitudes, and in exhibitions of their work often shocked the party functionaries. Such artists often promoted a progressive and expressively advanced form of critical realism and an aesthetics of their own making. The national contemporary art exhibitions, which took place every five years in Dresden, drew huge numbers of visitors from all over the country and provoked heated discussions.

We now know that the CIA was, at the height of the Cold War, instrumental in promoting abstract art in the West as a counterweight to 'communist' realism.[41] The CIA was able to capitalise on the fact that abstract art was frowned upon by party leaderships throughout the communist-led world where realist art was seen as better able to represent socialist values. This led to an often artificial polarisation between realist and abstract art, the former characterised in the West as old fashioned and conservative, the latter as progressive and representing individual freedom.

Not surprisingly, it meant a marginalisation of realist art in the West and a dominance of the abstract. The fact that much of the so-called 'socialist realist' art to which those in the West had access was state-commissioned and often second rate should not lead us to ignore the fact that there were excellent realist artists working in the Eastern bloc.

The country could also boast a number of artists, writers and scientists of international renown: the physicist, Manfred von Ardenne, the social scientist, Jürgen Kuczynski; visual artists like Fritz Kühn, John Heartfield, Willi Sitte, Werner Tübke and Wolfgang Mattheuer; writers like Christa Wolf, Stefan Hermlin, Stefan Heym, Christoph Hein, Erik

Neutsch and Erwin Strittmatter were all much admired beyond the GDR's borders.

In the theatre, Bertolt Brecht was, of course, the most famous. His influence on theatre practice was extensive in the GDR but also worldwide. The country, certainly in the early years, could also count on the expertise of actors and directors from the pre-Nazi period: Wolfgang Langhof, Wolf Kaiser, Wolfgang Heinz, Fritz Bennewitz and the brilliant Austrian opera director, Walther Felsenstein – people would come from all over the world to see his exciting productions at the Komische Oper in East Berlin.

Among those who matured post-war, Heiner Müller was widely recognised as one of Germany's most innovative and radical playwrights.

There were rock and pop bands like Silly and the Puhdys and jazz groups who were certainly not 'mouthpieces' of state-sanctioned culture. There was also a whole range of individual classical musicians of world class, like the conductor Kurt Masur, tenor Peter Schreier and baritone Olaf Bär, the chanteuse Gisela May as well as outstanding orchestras.

The GDR provided facilities and funding for artistic and creative theory and practice. There were lay art circles in most communities and these received state support to carry out their work. Many writers, musicians and visual artists enjoyed a quite privileged existence if they belonged to the officially recognised artists' or writers' associations. They would be offered regular well-paid commissions by state and local authorities which provided them, as creative artists, with an income to live on.

A number of leading writers were seen in many ways as 'people's tribunes', articulating grievances, criticisms and ideas that people felt had no proper airing in the public sphere. People engaged actively with these writers and vice versa. Public readings by, and discussions with, authors were a regular feature of GDR life.

Another myth constantly perpetuated is that because the GDR restricted the import of and access to literature from the West, its citizens were entirely cut off from it. A range of works by many contemporary writers from the West were published in the GDR; in fact more British authors were published there than authors from both Germanies combined were published in Britain. GDR readers could find books by British writers like Graham Greene, Harold Pinter and Alan Sillitoe to US writers like Saul Bellow, Norman Mailer and Ernest Hemingway. By 1981, the GDR was publishing 6,000 books a year, almost 17 per cent of which were translations from around 40 foreign languages.[42] There was a wide selection of international literature available and a number of foreign films were shown in cinemas. David Childs, in his book on East Germany,[43] exposes the myth that the GDR populace was totally ignorant and ill-informed about life in the West; most of them, after all were also able to tune in daily to West German radio and television.

Media

Radio and television in the GDR were owned by the state and there were strict guidelines imposed by the ruling party. However, that did not mean that people could only read, watch and hear one-dimensional propaganda from TV, film, radio and press. While news reporting was heavily controlled by the SED, there was a multitude of programmes that offered entertainment, education, debate and information.

The GDR had two TV channels which broadcast a wide range of material: news programmes, including special programmes on national affairs as well as international politics, magazine programmes about health, law and education, gardening, cooking, nature, advice for parents, sexual politics, sport, fashion, DIY, science and technology and cinema films. There were of course also special programmes for children and for young people, including the very popular daily bedtime story, brought by the puppet Sandmännchen (Sandman) adored by every generation. Entertainment was a large part of the schedule, especially music programmes but also police stories (often based on real incidents, which made them very believable and provided insights into every-day conflicts) and a whole range of television serials. GDR TV also produced a range of films, both historical and about contemporary life, of outstanding quality. Thus, the six-part series *Wege über's Land* (Paths across the country) showed the development of a village from 1914 until 1950, covering important periods of German history and its impact on the people. There were also excellent biopics of historical figures like J. S. Bach and Martin Luther to name just two.

There were several radio stations, one for news and entertainment, one for predominantly cultural and educational programmes, one for teenagers, and a local one for and about the capital Berlin and one international station, broadcasting in several languages providing information about the GDR.

The youth station, DT64 (named after the 1964 national youth festival, when the station was first launched) incorporated world music, with a high level of live performance which initiated a series of DT64 youth concerts. The station's broadcasting hours were regularly increased, eventually to 20 hours a day beginning at four in the morning with a rock music programme; on Saturdays international hits including a selection from West German, US and British pop charts were broadcast.

The world of newspaper and magazine publishing in the GDR was much broader then people in the West often assume. In fact, 1,770 different newspapers, magazines and journals with a total circulation of around 40 million were published. For children alone, there were 18 papers and magazines; there were also 500 specialist journals and 22 theological and religious publications. There were eight national newspapers, the largest being the one published by the Socialist Unity Party (SED), but there were also the ones from the other four parties in the GDR – the Christian Democratic Union (CDU), the National Democratic Party (NPDP), the Liberal Democratic Party (LDPD) and the Farmers Party – as well as papers published by the Free German Youth (FDJ), the Trade Union (FDGB) and the German Sports Association (DTSB). In addition, there were 29 regional newspapers – a strong tradition in Germany.

The GDR government saw the role of the media as a means of educating its citizens and winning them to the idea of socialism. Therefore radio, television, film and newspapers were subject to monitoring and censorship by the SED leadership. However, that did not mean a lack of quality reporting, programming and feature writing. It was always a battle of wits and the testing of boundaries between journalists and film-makers vis à vis the party leadership. But while most media coverage of news events was largely pedestrian and in accordance with the viewpoints and policies of the SED, there were many other areas where a broad spectrum of journalism could flourish. Particularly popular was the weekly *Der Sonntag*, published by the Kulturbund, because of its explorative essays and wide coverage of cultural events as well as discussions of different ways of life. A critique of real life in the GDR, albeit of a mild sort, was expressed usually through listeners' letters, but also in the popular magazine-style TV programme *Prisma*.

Many people in the country, including members of the ruling party, were often frustrated about the narrow parameters of the GDR's news coverage and supply of information through the media – but the leadership was unwilling to listen and respond. In the end, the SED's strict media policies proved to be more counter-productive than effective.

Most citizens were well informed despite the censored coverage of world news and rose-tinted internal reporting, largely because there was the possibility of receiving West German broadcasts on television and radio, which could be contrasted with what was said in the GDR's own media. People could thus compare and evaluate and in this way obtain a more balanced picture.

The GDR had its own film studios and produced a considerable number of feature and documentary films. Feature film productions, documentaries and historical series on television were often of a high quality. Thus the film *Jakob der Lügner* (Jacob the Liar), directed by Frank Beyer, was nominated for best foreign language film at the Academy Awards, and Rainer Simon's 1985 film *Die Frau und der Fremde* (The Woman and the Stranger) won the Golden Bear award at the 35th (West) Berlin International Festival. Children's films were also of a very high standard, particularly dramatisations of fairy tales and cartoon films. There were also a number of co-productions with other countries, like the film, based on Arthur Miller's play, *Die Hexen von Salem* (The Witches of Salem), starring Yves Montand and Simone Signoret.

A lot has been written about the films that were banned in the GDR. This did happen and was a sign of the narrow-mindedness of the party leadership which feared criticism. So it is by no means an endorsement of GDR censorship to point out that such activity was not confined to one part of Germany only. The FRG had its own forms of political censorship which were invariably used to hide and cover up the reporting of Nazi atrocities. Thus, Lord Russell's renowned book, The *Scourge of the Swastika*, which detailed Nazi war crimes, was banned there.

Film scripts were vetted and anything critical of Germany's recent Nazi past was censored. GDR films and books were banned as a matter of course. For instance, *Ein Tagebuch für Anne Frank* (A Diary for Anne Frank) by

Joachim Hellwig as well as Andrew and Annelie Thorndike's world-renowned documentary about the rise of Nazism in Germany, *Du und mancher Kamerad* (You and a few Comrades) and Wolfgang Staudte's classic film of the Heinrich Mann novel, *Der Untertan*.[44] These are just three of the many that were banned from being shown in West Germany. Even the great Italian director, Vittoria de Sica's film *I sequestrati di Altona* (The Condemned of Altona), based on Sartre's *Huis Clos*, was censored and all references to the Nazis removed.

Alain Resnais' short documentary, *Nuit et Brouillard* (Night and Fog) about the Nazi concentration camps, made to commemorate the 10th anniversary of the end of the war, was condemned by the West German government and it made an official complaint to the French government that showing the film 'would be an obstacle to the reconciliation of the two peoples'. As a result, the film was withdrawn from competition at the Cannes Film Festival under much protest.

During the first five years of the Federal Republic the public screening of several hundred films were banned for political reasons, but the files relating to this are still secret. This was all part of the post-war ideological struggle, the inevitable clash of the two systems, but this aspect is conveniently forgotten today.

In the short period between the fall of the Wall (on 9 November 1989) and the accession of the GDR to the Federal Republic (on 3 October 1990) when the GDR still existed, the media enjoyed an unprecedented freedom from both party dictates and commercial pressures. Journalists relished their new freedom and audiences enjoyed access to a wide range of different perspectives.

GDR journalists proved that they were not only supremely capable of reporting the truth and investigating news stories, but were also able to run their own media institutions with competence. With unification, this era came to an abrupt stop: television and radio stations were taken over or closed down, as were film studios and newspapers. Most journalists and film-makers were purged and lost their jobs.

Following the currency union in July 1990, almost all GDR publishing houses were closed and half a million freshly printed books were pulped, including those by classical authors, works of writers exiled by fascism, coffee-table volumes and even Bach scores. Most of those GDR authors who had been lauded in the West over the years for their critical writings were suddenly of no interest anymore and were dropped like hot potatoes by new owners rapidly moving into the book selling business.

Sport

Mass sport in the GDR enjoyed high status. Sport among citizens of all ages was very popular and was subsidised by the state; the promotion of sport was even anchored in the constitution. According to the statutory regulations covering work, all employees were allowed time off to take part in sporting activities, if it was not possible to do it outside work time. Under the law, sporting injuries were given the same legal status as workplace accidents.

The GDR state leadership made consistent attempts to promote and maintain the strong German working class sporting tradition. Its first prime minister, Walter Ulbricht, himself followed his own 1959 slogan, 'Everyone everywhere – once a week sport'; he went ice skating and skiing, played volleyball and table tennis and even took part in public sporting events.

In schools, two to three hours per week were devoted to sport education. Even in colleges and universities sport was obligatory for all students for at least a year although they could choose which sport they wanted to do. In schools, sport was not just a question of playing games; athletics and gymnastics, including exercises on various items of sports equipment, games and swimming were all part of the curriculum. In addition, many children and young people were given the opportunity of partaking in after-school sports activities.

There were around 11,000 amateur sports clubs in the country of which membership was usually free. For the most talented youngsters, special sports schools were available where specialist training was offered in addition to the normal curriculum.

Every year, there were sports competitions organised at district, regional and national level which were very popular. For example, in 1983, almost a million children and young people took part in regional summer games and more than 30,000 in winter games. These competitions were highly motivating for those taking part and were also an effective means for talent spotting. From 1950 onwards, a special sporting award, available in gold, silver and bronze, was introduced. Qualification for the awards was based on age group and the most popular sports were swimming, running, jumping, discus and javelin, shot-put and gymnastics.

Through the media, attempts were made to get everyone involved in sport. In one weekly sports programme, for example, teams from schools in various towns would compete with each other in sporting events and each year an overall winner would receive a cup. These kinds of competitions generated enormous enthusiasm. Shortly after the fall of the Wall, East and West German school teams competed against each other in a similar way, but the East German teams easily beat their West German peers. The programme was taken off air in 1991 when GDR television was closed down.

The sporting field was an area in which the GDR

excelled and produced world-class sports men and women in surprising numbers given its small population. In the last Olympic Games in which the GDR took part, in Seoul, it won 37 gold, 35 silver and 30 bronze medals. Since its demise much publicity has been given to the use of performance enhancing drugs and the misuse of steroids as a means of explaining away the GDR's sports achievements. While some abuse undoubtedly took place, it would be nonsense to accept that this alone explained the GDR's sporting successes. As we now know very well, the abuse and use of steroids was and still is widespread throughout the sporting world.

What gives the lie to the accusation that the GDR's sports trainers were merely 'drug pushers' is the fact that, after unification, in successive winter and summer Olympic Games as well as in world competitions, the lion's share of medals for Germany still went to former GDR sportsmen and women.

Take the example of Heike Drechsler , one of the most successful female long jumpers of all time who also had a number of successes in sprint disciplines and is the only woman to have won two Olympic gold medals in the long jump (1992 and 2000). As a teenager she was active in the FDJ and in 1984 was elected to the GDR parliament. She continued to have a distinguished athletic career after unification and never failed a doping test. Katharina Witt, the GDR's most popular figure skater, also won two gold medals in the winter Olympics and went on to star in her own ice show in the USA and appeared in several films after unification. She also headed Munich's (unsuccessful) bid to host the 2018 winter Olympics.

Many of the GDR's sports trainers went on to work with national sporting organisations in a number of countries around the world, including the USA, Australia, Austria, Switzerland and the Federal Republic itself, where their methodology was effective and their genuine abilities were valued and trusted. The vilification of GDR sporting achievement and its dismissal as merely the result of drug use did not appear to worry these countries too much when it came to promoting their own teams' success.[45]

FREEDOM AND DEMOCRACY

In the West, freedom and democracy have always been largely defined as the right to vote within a multi-party system and to act and speak relatively unrestrained; but it does not include the right to be free *from* something e.g. homelessness or unemployment. By Western definition none of the socialist countries was really democratic or free, even though elections were held. However, freedom and democracy cannot be adequately defined or encapsulated in such a simplistic manner.

True freedom and democracy involves much more than voting and choosing between ostensibly different parties at election times. They are found in the interstices of life – in our work, social and family life, in the range of opportunities available to us in order to fulfil our potential, on a daily basis, how much control we have over our own lives and how accountable to us our representatives are. Such basic human rights as freedom from fear and the right to housing, to water, health, education and to adequate nourishment are included in the UN Charter. A freedom simply to vote cannot alone substitute for such basic and vital freedoms. As Paul Ginsborg puts it, 'If citizens share equal rights in the political sphere, but are highly unequal in the economic one, then democracy is likely to be deeply flawed.'[46]

The constitution of the GDR incorporated such rights as the right to work and, to a considerable degree, to choose one's place of work depending on appropriate professional qualification and social requirement, the right to housing, guaranteed equal pay for equal work, the right to education and training and the right to state-supported care in old age, to name some of the most important.

Even though there were five political parties everyone knew that the real power lay with the ruling Socialist Unity Party (SED) and the other parties were largely subservient to it. The leading role of the SED was actually written into the constitution. That meant that even though these several parties existed, there was no official or recognised opposition in parliament. All parties stood in elections and acted as a bloc called 'The National Front' (a name reflecting the feeling of being under continual threat from the West during the Cold War). However, the composition of parliament was not based on party strengths alone; only two thirds of seats were designated for members of the parties and one third was taken by delegates from non-party mass organisations with the largest memberships being the FDGB (trade union federation), DFD (Democratic German Women's Association), the FDJ (the national youth organisation) and Kulturbund (the Cultural Association).

People's democratic rights in their communities and their workplaces were considerable and they could, in this way, often directly influence affairs that impinged directly on their lives. Most local issues, whether concerning building and planning, cultural issues or the organisation of public events, were usually open to public debate. While democratic rights, as understood in the West, were limited in the GDR, there was wide participation in democratic processes at grassroots level. For instance during the public discussions around the formulation of a new family law, over 33,000 public meetings took place up and down the country to discuss the proposed new legislation. There were also regular discussions in the press and on radio. A similar process took place during deliberations around the introduction of a new constitution in 1968 and around the draft of new legislation on the rights of young people in 1974.

Yet, what galled people was the almost paranoid fear by the SED leadership and the security services of anti-state activities, rebellion and counter-revolution which led to them suspecting everyone of being potential enemy agents. The leadership never really felt secure and instead of gradually endowing more trust in the people as the country developed and became more mature, it never shed its distrust of its own citizens. While few would question the state's essential role in protecting itself and the country from outside subversion, many did resent the over-emphasis on the need for security. Those who openly questioned or challenged the Party's right to leadership would invariably be deemed disloyal and even suspect. While most ordinary working people were hardly affected by such demands, intellectuals and artists definitely were. Their battles for free expression and for the right to individual creativity were often bitter and harsh. A whole number were unable to accept or deal with such interference and suffered from depression and stress, and several left the country. This aspect of what was essentially a one-party state but also one in which the Soviet Union continually interfered and insisted on its example being followed in almost all areas had seriously negative consequences on how socialism in the GDR evolved.

Given this uncomfortable situation for so many, one might legitimately ask why more intellectuals and artists did not oppose the government and party leadership more strongly or even leave for the West. To attempt to understand why they did not, it is necessary to comprehend that most genuinely believed in a socialist society and despite all the restrictions and deformations, hoped for a gradual reform and democratisation. especially in the wake of Stalin's death and the Krushchev reforms, but also with the Helsinki Accords in 1975 and Gorbachev's election in 1985.

One of the greatest sources of bitterness and frustration for GDR citizens were the travel restrictions. People were able to travel to Eastern European countries and even, in restricted numbers, to Cuba. It was, though, hardly possible to make private trips to western countries, unless one were on official business. Western media have made much of the stories of individuals escaping or attempting to leave the GDR, sometimes employing quite adventurous means, but what they did not mention was that between 1961, when the Wall was built, and 1989, when the Wall came down, more than 429,000 people officially moved to the West, i.e. with permission from the GDR authorities.[47]

Travel restrictions, though, were not imposed by one side only. In the early years of the GDR right into the seventies, any GDR citizen wishing to travel to western countries had to apply for a visa through the Allied Travel Office in West Berlin. This office was an instrument of the Cold War and was used as a means of humiliating the GDR by selecting those to whom it was prepared to issue visas and denying or delaying those with whom it was not happy, particularly if they were considered in any way representatives of the state.

There were a number of valid reasons for the GDR's travel restrictions, not least a shortage of foreign currency, but also the fear of the country losing key professionals who could command far bigger salaries in the West.

From 1964, pensioners were permitted to travel once a year to relatives in the West. In 1975, the Helsinki Accords represented a significant rapprochement and a lowering of tensions throughout Europe, bringing about a genuine thawing of East-West relations. As a result, an increasing number of people below pensioner age were able to travel to West Germany to visit relatives. In 1986, one of the West German diplomats, who had resided and worked in the GDR, returned to Bonn and wrote, 'We had an increasing number of visitors ... This year, there were about 200,000 visitors who were below pensionable age from the GDR visiting the Federal Republic, something that we were very pleased about.'[48]

Justice and legal rights

In areas such as legal rights and justice, perhaps surprisingly to some, the GDR had much to offer in terms of looking at social alternatives to current structures of the justice system. In the 1970s, the GDR undertook a complete re-writing of the country's Civil Code. The previous Civil Code of justice had been in place for over a hundred years and indeed some laws went back a lot further. Apart from hardly being appropriate for a modern state, the laws were couched in such archaic language that few ordinary people could understand them. It was decided to rewrite the Code and make it 'citizen friendly', i.e. comprehensible without the requirement of a degree in jurisprudence or recourse to a lawyer. Even today this Civil Code retains validity and relevance in terms of its innovative approach and the effective removal of layers of dusty, archaic jurisprudence: it re-empowered citizens to be in a position in which they could undertake much of their own legal administration. Yet, like all other GDR legislation, this Civil Code was rejected after unification and the old, complex and archaic (West) German one was re-imposed.

The GDR Code incorporated a system that provided citizens with the means of making complaints to local, regional and national authorities if they felt they had been unjustly treated or that things that had happened to them were perceived as unfair. This was the 'Eingaben' system (complaints or petition procedure). It allowed individuals to ventilate their grievances, and civil servants at local, regional and national level were statutorily obliged to reply to such grievances and to address the issues raised within a fixed time frame. The Code also covered the work of the Conflict Commissions, which functioned as quasi lay magistrates courts, dealing with minor crimes or infringements whose role has been dealt with under the section on Workers' Rights.

Interestingly, as early as 1956, the GDR had abolished paragraph 175 of the German penal code which outlawed homosexuality, but even beforehand the law had been largely ignored. This was probably facilitated by the fact that the GDR was an overwhelmingly atheistic state. In the Federal Republic, between 1945 and 1969, around 50,000 men were convicted of homosexual practice.[49] It was not until 1969 that the FRG eventually abolished the persecution of homosexuals.

Even if the GDR justice system was far from perfect and injustices, in terms of the treatment of political dissidents, did take place, to characterise the country as a whole as an 'Unrechtsstaat' (an unjust state or one without justice), as the leaders of the new Germany do, is to misrepresent reality.

Religious freedom

In 1950, around 85 per cent of GDR citizens had belonged nominally to a Protestant church and 10 per cent were Catholics. Forty years later, these figures had decreased significantly: only 25 per cent were now Protestant and 5 per cent Catholic. The proportion of those belonging to no confession rose from 6 to 70 per cent by 1989.

The role and stature of religion in the GDR changed radically over the 40 years of the state's existence. As indicated by the figures above, the vast majority of GDR citizens, certainly in its later years, did not belong to any faith grouping. However, religious institutions existed and religious leaders were free to carry out their pastoral work. Those who wished to join a religious organisation and go to church could do so without let or hindrance. State organisations, though, made it clear that they encouraged secularism.

In the country, there were many Christian churches, several denominations of Protestant and Roman Catholic, and even some small groups of Mormons, Seventh Day Adventists and Quakers. There was also a small Jewish community. Somewhat surprisingly perhaps, 22 religious newspapers and magazines were published in the country.

Traditionally, and pre-war, the churches had been, with a few honourable exceptions, very conservative and invariably anti-socialist, and many had also largely tolerated if not actively supported the Nazi regime. They maintained close links with their partner churches in the Federal Republic from whom they also received financial support for purposes like church renovation. It is therefore perhaps not surprising that the church and religious organisations in general were often viewed by the state with some suspicion.

However, churches were free to hold services and meetings with parishioners, and religious leaders could carry out their religious responsibilities with little or no harassment; some co-operated closely with the SED and organs of state where they felt it helpful. There was even a ministry for religious affairs whose express purpose was to liaise with the churches and one of the parties represented in parliament was the Christian Democratic Party (CDU). On issues like the struggle for peace, international solidarity and anti-racism, there was often co-operation between religious organisations and the government. Christian churches also ran and maintained a number of hospitals and care homes with government co-operation.

Religion was not taught in schools and its place was taken by a lesson on ethics and social responsibility. There was an understanding between state and religious institutions that the state would not interfere in their affairs and the churches would confine their activities to religion and not meddle in matters of the state.

In this context, it is worth mentioning that the present Chancellor of Germany, Angela Merkel, is the daughter of a Protestant pastor and theologian who, in 1954, a few weeks after the birth of his daughter, moved from Hamburg to live in the GDR, where he settled in the small Mecklenburg town of Templin. It seems despite any misgivings he may have had or even disagreements with the government, that joining the attempt to build a socialist society was more in keeping with his Christian principles than living and working in a capitalist West Germany. In 1963, he was appointed to a leading position in a Protestant seminary. Although very much a committed Christian, he did not adopt an oppositional position towards the GDR. He clearly felt his religion and his work as a clergyman within the GDR were compatible.

One of the curious consequences of unification is the fact that there are now roadside signs giving the times of church services at the entrance to every village and town, in accordance with West German practice – even though the East Germans are overwhelmingly secular. According to one of the most recent surveys,[50] more than three quarters of the population in the former GDR still profess not to belong to any religious group. This shows that figures have not changed since 1989.

The State Security Services

The name 'Stasi' has now been adopted worldwide as the quintessential short-term description of an extremely oppressive and brutal police state. But what was the reality of the GDR's Security Service (Stasi for short)?

After the war, before the GDR came into being, East German security was undertaken by the Soviet Union and the KGB. Most of their activities in those early years involved tracking down and convicting leading Nazis and those who had committed war crimes.

Hitler's former chief security officer on the Eastern Front, Major General Reinhard Gehlen, was recruited in

1946 by the USA largely because of his detailed knowledge of the Soviet Union and of communist activities. Gehlen offered the US his intelligence archives and his network of contacts in return for his freedom and that of his colleagues. He handpicked 350 former Nazi agents to join him, a number that eventually grew to 4,000 undercover agents. This group soon acquired the sobriquet 'Gehlen Organisation'. When the 'Iron Curtain' was drawn in 1946, leaving the Western allies with virtually no intelligence sources in Eastern Europe, Gehlen's vast store of knowledge made him very valuable.

He went on to head West Germany's intelligence organisation, the BND, until 1968. The BND had a clear anti-communist focus right from the start, and the organisation was populated by many former Nazis. It was hardly surprising that the GDR felt threatened.

In response to the employment of former top Nazis in the West, the Soviet Union felt obliged to set up its own East German security organisation which then morphed into the GDR's Ministry of State Security in 1950.

Just as the USA has its FBI and CIA and Britain its MI5 and MI6 (plus Special Branch and the Metropolitan Police Anti-terrorist Branch), the GDR security service had two arms – the counter espionage section headed by Markus Wolf and the internal security section headed by Erich Mielke. Markus Wolf was a highly cultured Jewish intellectual, the son of Friedrich Wolf, a medical doctor and anti-fascist who was also a renowned playwright; Markus was also the brother of Konrad Wolf, one of the GDR's most talented and respected film directors. Mielke came from a working class background and was a communist already in the pre-Hitler days, spending the Nazi years in Soviet exile; he was an old style, hard-line communist.

The central role of all security agencies – and the GDR was no different – was to protect the state from attempts to undermine or destabilise it. The early years of the GDR, until 1961, with its still open border to West Berlin, were marked by acts of sabotage by those opposed to it as well as infiltration by Western spy agencies, as so graphically depicted in the novels of John le Carré. The GDR state security forces had their work cut out simply dealing with such issues.

Its counter-espionage arm was one of the most effective and successful agencies of any state; it penetrated deep into NATO headquarters and even the West German Chancellor's office. After the demise of the GDR, its chief, Markus Wolf, was put on trial, found guilty of treason and given a six-year prison sentence for carrying out espionage against the Federal Republic. This was quite grotesque since, after all, this had been his job – but it demonstrated that the FRG had never recognised the GDR as a sovereign state, despite its place in the UN and world-wide recognition by other states. Wolf's conviction was later quashed by the German supreme court. Wolf said that, shortly before unification, the CIA had offered him a seven-figure sum and a new identity in California if he were willing to work for them – something he spurned.

Markus Wolf, long before he retired in 1986, had become disillusioned by the intransigence of the ossified leadership in the country. Through his work as the GDR's chief of counter espionage, he had acquired a comprehensive and differentiated view of the world and could see that change was desperately needed if the GDR were to survive. He became one of those who threw their full weight behind the reform movement during the late eighties.

When reviewing the role of the security services responsible for internal security in the GDR, one has to take account of the changing historical circumstances during the country's existence. There is no doubt that in the early years, in which the Soviet Union played a dominant role, serious breaches of democratic norms took place. With the increased stabilisation of the GDR and certainly after the closing of its borders, the security services adopted a less confrontational and panic-led role.

The internal wing of the State Security Services, and it is this wing that is commonly referred to as the Stasi today, was primarily concerned with nipping in the bud any group or individual activity which it deemed threatening to the stability of the state. Most of its activities involved surveillance and sometimes the threat of punitive action. Those seen as undermining the state were indeed arrested and convicted for political actions that in most Western democratic states would be deemed legal and permissible. Even an application to emigrate to the West was considered an 'unfriendly act' and would invariably incur repercussions, even though thousands, often after delays and bureaucratic procedures, were allowed to emigrate.

Over the years, several people were convicted and imprisoned for political activities, but most of the sentences were for several months or a few years, rarely for very long periods. A number of these prisoners also had their prison sentences curtailed when they were exchanged for GDR agents imprisoned in West Germany or for hard currency; others were simply expelled from the country on release. Several political dissidents who served their sentences were given the opportunity of reintegrating into society.

Few of us would deny the security services a key role in combatting terrorism or the threat of violence by any organisation or individual to further their political aims, but many of us would balk at the use of the security services to undermine democratic rights or peaceful protest, which the Stasi certainly did.

Despite depictions to the contrary, the Stasi was not a force unto itself, it operated under the guidance of the Party leadership and was always subject to Party control. It rarely operated in an arbitrary or gratuitous manner of its own accord. That said, it was undoubtedly a powerful and oppressive force within the state, because it was used to enforce compliance by intimidation rather than persuasion and political argument.

One example of such oppressive action by the Stasi against a democratic organisation was that taken against the movement 'Swords into Ploughshares', which utilised an image of the famous Soviet sculpture of the same title. The organisation emerged in the GDR in the early 1980s, at a time when the US was stationing cruise missiles in the FRG and the Soviet Union responded by stationing SS20 rockets in the GDR. The organisation championed pacifism, disarmament and opposed the global weapons industry. It was a movement initiated and supported by church organisations and pacifists. Because of its sane argumentation it gained rapid support, but the state feared its popularity could lead to an undermining of its defence policy and encourage young men to become conscientious objectors and refuse to serve in the armed forces – at this time both Germanies still had conscription.

So how did the Stasi react to the 'Swords into Ploughshares' movement? It put pressure on church officials to curb the organisation's activity, it got schools and colleges to ban the wearing of the badge or the displaying of posters. Individual youngsters – those involved were mainly young – who refused to be cowed and were determined to confront the authorities, were threatened with or, in some cases, actually were expelled from school or college or not allowed to sit their exams.

Several who took part in demonstrations or pickets were even given short custodial sentences. While this Stasi action was clearly a breach of democratic procedure and an abuse of human rights, its action could hardly be characterised as extreme brutality. But it was exactly this sort of action that the Stasi usually resorted to, using pressure and threats to achieve its aims.

The security services did flout democratic norms,

undertook action that was illegal, even in terms of the GDR's constitution – but, as we know today, this seems to be in the nature of all security services. What remains a fact though is that the Stasi was an organisation that carried out a humiliating monitoring of all sections of society and, in the name of protecting the state, suppressed almost any oppositional activity or action it deemed would undermine the security of the state.

The impression has been deliberately fostered that there was nationwide surveillance by the Stasi, and that everybody was spying on everybody else, that no one could even tell a political joke without being informed on and arrested. In actual fact, only 2 per cent of the population was involved in Stasi activities – and that includes full-time employees and informants – according to official data disclosed by Roger Engelmann, Project Director of the Federal German institution for the investigation of the Stasi files. So, the much-publicised 'total surveillance' system, fell far short of such a description.

Since unification, the German government has spared no effort or expense to investigate what it calls 'crimes' of the GDR. The Enquete Kommission (Commission of Enquiry) established by the government and given the task of investigating the 'SED dictatorship' detailed a series of victim categories for which evidence was to be sought. These were: deaths in custody, contract assassinations by the state both inside the GDR and abroad, rendition to foreign powers, murder with the collaboration of medics, the withholding of necessary medical aid and forced adoptions.[51]

As a result, around 30,000 cases were opened by public prosecutors against former employees of the Stasi. In the end, 20 individuals were found guilty, of whom 12 were given fines and seven suspended sentences. Chief prosecutor Schaefgen was unable to find a single case of torture, the use of radioactive radiation, of pharmacological drugs, the administering of electrical shocks or similar torture methods. This meagre outcome was certainly not for want of strenuous effort. There is a huge chasm between the lurid stories spread by the media and the facts themselves; but despite this, the same accusations are continually regurgitated.

For example, one of the big West German tabloid newspapers reported that in Stasi prisons more than 2,500 prisoners were murdered and thousands committed suicide. In reality, nobody was murdered and in almost four decades, 14 suicides took place in all the holding prisons of the State Security apparatus.[52]

It is also true that corruption was not a characteristic of the Stasi in the sense that it appears to be today in many police forces, even in the so-called democratic states.

In contrast to the Stasi files, West German secret service (BND) files relating to the Nazi past are still kept under lock and key. In 2012, the Linke parliamentary group in the Bundestag requested that BND files on the Nazis be made accessible. At the same time, the party also asked the government to release all files concerning any collaboration and possible obstruction of due judicial process in the prosecution of Nazi war criminals. These requests were denied – even the files relating to top Nazi, Adolf Eichmann, remain secret.

Another commonly cited statistic is that 180km of shelving is apparently needed to hold all Stasi documents and is continually reiterated by the authorities. You have to delve assiduously in order to find out what is actually contained in these kilometers of documentation. They include: files on individuals requesting official recognition as 'victims of fascism', documents about the Nazi period, about the Eastern offices of those parties – SPD, CDU and LDPD – re-established after the war, reparations paid to the Soviet Union, Soviet military tribunals and other judicial papers, information about the GDR and the West German armies, counter intelligence reports, exchange of agents, information on Western spy agencies, applications for permission to emigrate, foreign relations maintained by the parties, verbatim transcripts from Western agencies and ministries, details of town twinning between the GDR and FRG, property ownership details, survey reports on 'attitudes of the population', materials about housing, workplace rights, problems of food supply, imports that were made despite the Western embargo, monitoring of terrorist and extremist groups around the world, nuclear security and protection against radiation, environmental problems, CVs of those permitted to travel to the West, security measures for teams going to the Olympic Games ... Much of it appears to be normal run-of-the-mill documentation that any state authority would keep.[53]

Both within and outside Germany the image of the GDR as an 'unjust/illegal state' in which every citizen was either intimidated by the Stasi or kept under surveillance by them or both, has been firmly cemented in the consciousness with the result that the GDR today has become synonymous with the word Stasi . But those who argue that the organisation penetrated all aspects of life, ignore the memories of most of those who lived in the GDR. Their assertions invariably provoke tedium, prickliness and defiance in the latter. If, as a GDR citizen, you were not a dissident nor expressed opposition to the state or socialism as a concept, you would probably have had little or no contact with the Stasi throughout your life. But if you did express opposition or were critical – as many artists by the very nature of their work were – then you would probably have had dealings with it. However, the Stasi was hardly the monstrous all-seeing, omnipotent vicious organisation it has been depicted.

INTERNATIONALISM AND FOREIGN AID

The GDR's record on internationalism was exemplary and it took the idea of solidarity with other, struggling nations seriously. Undoubtedly the internationalism demonstrated by German communists before the Second World War, in solidarity with the Soviet Union and particularly the role they played in Spain during the 1930s, also had some influence on its foreign policy. A number of ex-International Brigaders held leading positions in party and state.

Many of the struggles of colonial and former colonial countries for liberation and national independence received vital material and political support. The GDR sent doctors and other medical staff to the front line in Vietnam, Mozambique, Angola and other countries. It provided logistical support and training for SWAPO, the movement for independence in Namibia, as well as to the ANC in South Africa, printing *Sechaba*, its official newsletter for many years.

Numerous foreign students from countries struggling to free themselves from the legacy of colonialism were given free training and education in the GDR itself. Refuge was also offered to those fleeing oppressive regimes; many Chileans in enforced exile from Pinochet's fascist regime found asylum there, including its current president, Michelle Bachelet.

Work and solidarity brigades organised by the GDR's youth organisation, the FDJ, helped young, newly independent states and those still fighting for independence to build up their infrastructures – factories, schools, hospitals and the establishment of vocational training centres. Between 1964 and 1988, there were 60 friendship brigades made up of around 1,000 young people working in 26 countries of Africa, Asia and Latin America. In Algeria a brigade built houses for the homeless, in Mali they trained agricultural workers, in Nicaragua they built a training school for mechanics and, in 1980, a hospital financed in large part by donations made by GDR citizens. By September 1985, the Karl Marx hospital, as it was named, had treated 10,000 patients, among them 3,000 children, and another 10,000 were supplied with medicines. The hospital is still working today, but now under the more innocuous name of 'German-Nicaraguan Hospital'. In 2005 it celebrated its 25th anniversary.

International solidarity also became part of everyone's daily life: liberation struggles and detailed stories of life in less developed countries were reported in the media daily; in schools and colleges, students learned about the struggles of people in other parts of the world, rather than merely talking about poverty and hunger. A number of GDR schools were named after leading freedom fighters including a Nelson Mandela school in Ilmenau which was immediately renamed in 1989 because Mandela was then still deemed to be a terrorist by the West German government.

The level of mass solidarity with Vietnam in the 1960s and 1970s was unprecedented, with voluntary regular contributions made in almost every workplace, blood donations organised by the FDJ and the building of a hospital in Vietnam, alongside other projects.

The GDR also signed agreements with North Vietnam and Mozambique whereby workers from the two countries came to the GDR to work on fixed-term contracts. They worked and were given training at the same time. Such agreements were mutually beneficial, as the GDR had a shortage of labour and Vietnam and Mozambique needed trained workers as well as foreign currency. Such agreements have since been criticised since as a form of 'indentured labour' or exploitation, but such a depiction is simply inaccurate.

It is also important to stress that although the GDR often reached mutually advantageous trade agreements with the countries to which it gave aid, much of its contribution, particularly to liberation struggles and poorer countries, was one-sided – aid was provided out of a genuine sense of internationalism not for economic gain. Even today people in countries like Namibia, South Africa and Mozambique still talk positively about the generous help they received from the GDR.

In terms of the GDR's impact internationally, its role in maintaining world peace should not be underestimated. Situated geographically on the front line between the two big power blocs, it often found itself sitting on a tinderbox. Any rash action or provocation on its part could have easily unleashed a new war in Europe. The GDR leadership was very much aware of this and fought consistently for peaceful co-existence and a rapprochement between the two Germanies – but not at the expense of giving up its attempt to build socialism.

Over the period of its existence, the government made a whole number of overtures to the West in an attempt to normalise relations and defuse the almost permanent confrontational situation on its border.

After the election in 1969 of the Social Democratic Chancellor, Willi Brandt, who was more amenable to dialogue, new policies by both sides brought a tentative easing of tension. It led to both Brandt and Honecker paying official visits to their respective states. Even under Helmut Kohl's conservative government relations improved during the 1980s culminating in Honecker's official visit to the FRG in 1987, where the government greeted him with the full protocol honours appropriate for an official state visit and thus tacitly accepting the sovereignty of the GDR as well as the two-state reality of Germany. However, once the Wall came down, Kohl saw his chance of incorporating the GDR into an enlarged Germany. In all later negotiations with the Soviet Union about the future of the GDR Kohl negotiated as if speaking for all Germans and ignored the requests made by the interim Modrow government for the GDR to be treated as an equal partner in negotiations around unification.[54]

THE DEMISE OF THE GDR

The fall of the Wall

The reader may well ask: if life in the GDR had so many positive aspects as described here, why did so many, particularly young people, wish to leave for the West and why did a majority vote for unification in the 1990 elections? There is no simple answer to that, but there are a number of influential factors.

We have described the increasing frustration with the ossified and intransigent leadership and the over-centralisation of decision-making, the increasing chasm between the government and the people. During the autumn of 1989, there was an explosion of democratic grassroot initiatives that were openly demanding a proper say in decision-making. Several civil rights organisations were established (e.g. Neues Forum, Demokratie Jetzt, Demokratischer Aufbruch) and weekly demonstrations began in Leipzig, then in other towns in October 1989 all demanding change.

The dominant slogans were 'We are the People' and 'We are staying here' (as a reaction to those who were leaving the GDR via the Hungarian border which had been opened in the summer of 1989). This pressure from the people, forced the resignation of Erich Honecker, general secretary of the SED and head of state, in October 1989. But when a new head of state was again selected from the existing nomenclatura, the demonstrations continued unabated. Moreover, public discussions started taking place in many big cities about what an improved socialism should or could look like, what needed to be changed to make it more open and democratic and give citizens a stronger voice in the decision-making process. At that time, the media started to change as well and journalists demonstrated courage and imagination in tackling difficult subject matters. Programmes on radio and television were introduced that reflected the sudden explosion of debate and many of the topics being voiced by the people were discussed in the media.

There is still some controversy about how and why the Wall was opened in the way it was, i.e. not through a formal and prepared announcement. What the GDR government had been planning was the introduction of a new law easing travel restrictions on GDR citizens wishing to visit the West. And when the question was asked at a government press conference on 9 November 1989, as to when this new law would come into force the answer, after some hesitation, was 'with immediate effect'. It will remain one of the mysteries of history whether this was incompetence or a deliberate act of sabotage. The fact remains that the West German media immediately broadcast this announcement and GDR citizens, with some disbelief, rushed to the border in Berlin to see for themselves whether it was true. The West reacted very quickly and offered every GDR citizen crossing the border 100 Deutsch Marks that were promptly spent in the consumer temples of West Berlin.

Shortly after the opening of the borders, the GDR government resigned and was replaced by an interim government under the popular former Dresden Regional Secretary of the SED, Hans Modrow. He formed a new government including all the five GDR parties and worked closely together with the 'Central Round Table', that was formed in early December 1989, bringing together the established parties, mass organisations and the new civil rights movements.

Only 13 days after the Wall was opened, the governing board of the West German central bank proposed the rapid introduction of the West German currency in the GDR. It was a plan aimed at buying the revolution. The battle for the future of the GDR began with Helmut Kohl's speech in the Bundestag on 28 November 1989, in which he proposed a path to unification. On the same day, leading GDR intellectuals and writers issued an appeal 'For our country', calling for a stand-alone GDR. At that time, 86 per cent of the GDR population wanted a reformed socialism.[55]

People's confidence in being able to create a separate reformed socialist state was systematically undermined by a mixture of lurid exposure stories and disinformation about the GDR's former rulers. In addition, the (West German) media began a propaganda war claiming that the GDR economy was near collapse and that the GDR government was within days of becoming insolvent and unable to pay its bills. All of a sudden Federal German flags appeared at the weekly demonstrations and gatherings, and the dominant slogan was changed to 'We are ONE people'. Modrow's government was increasingly sidelined by Helmut Kohl who now started direct negotiations with Mikhail Gorbachev on the feasibility of German unification.[56]

The planned general election date was brought forward from May to March 1990. These elections have been characterised as the GDR's 'first free elections' – and indeed elections in GDR times were not genuinely democratic. However, although the GDR was still a sovereign state and the Modrow 'government of national responsibility' and the parties and organisations represented in the Modrow government had agreed that there should be no interference by West German parties. But despite this there was heavy involvement by those parties in the election campaign, particularly the CDU.

Clearly, a lot was at stake for the West German CDU under Helmut Kohl. He had been in office already for two terms and his party's popularity was waning. Elections in the Federal Republic were due in December 1990. He saw his chance of fulfilling an old dream, namely re-uniting Germany and finally banishing the spectre of a socialist alternative in the shape of a separate state. The CDU, therefore, threw everything into the election battle in the GDR in order to convince the people that joining West Germany would give our 'poor brothers and sisters in the GDR' a panacea. That is why he promised 'blooming landscapes' and similar living standards to those in the West. Consumerism was the big draw under the slogan of freedom.

The powerful West German political parties, particularly the CDU, donated large sums of money, printed election propaganda and provided a free service of 'advisers' to their designated partners in the East.[57] According to a report now lodged in the archive of the Stiftung Deutsches Rundfunkarchiv (DRA), West German parties and prominent politicians gained increasing influence over the GDR's election process.

In total 7.5 million Deutsch Marks were spent on these campaigns in the GDR. Over half of that amount came from the CDU/CSU, which spent 4.5 million on the election campaign of its sister party in the GDR. The West German CDU was quite open about its attempts to influence the electoral process. Chancellor Kohl himself spoke at six big rallies, addressing an estimated one million citizens or 10 per cent of the GDR electorate. Alongside him, other leading CDU politicians also spoke at over a thousand electoral events. Everything, including television and radio, newspapers, posters and leaflets were mobilised to ensure a victory for the 'Allianz für Deutschland' – an alliance of the East German CDU and two minor right-wing parties that had been set up only six weeks before the election by Chancellor Kohl himself.

The West German CDU even produced a 16-page newspaper specifically for the election, in an edition of five million copies. The tenor of the campaign was twofold: to underline the 'We are One People' concept ('Wir sind ein Volk') and its anti-socialist stance, 'Never again Socialism' ('Nie wieder Sozialismus').[58]

Egon Bahr, then a member of the Executive Committee of the West German Social Democratic Party, immediately after election booths had closed on 18 March 1990, said:

> What I have seen during this period in the GDR made me extremely angry ... the whole election campaign became an event that was controlled by the West German CDU. It was an undignified operation ... loudspeaker vans with Munich-registered number plates swamped Leipzig's streets and called for people not to attend the SPD's election hustings ... in small towns in Thuringia and Saxony many known members of the SPD and PDS received threatening letters and were even physically assaulted ... children were given money to hand out leaflets on behalf of the CSU [the CDU's sister party in the West]. That was pure psychological terror in a Goebbels' mould. I wish to reiterate that this political dirt was imported from the Federal Republic.[59]

The result of the election was a shock for all those who had wanted a reformed GDR or, at best, a confederation with the Federal Republic. The 'Allianz für Deutschland' proposed that the GDR should become part of the Federal Republic by simply joining rather than negotiating a unification agreement. This policy was pursued in the following months by the newly elected GDR parliament which handed over its sovereignty even before an all-German parliament had been set up. 'Allianz für Deutschland' was the clear winner with 48 per cent of the votes, although most pundits had expected the SPD to come out on top.

All the GDR parties (apart from the Party of Democratic Socialism and the civil rights movement) had advisers from the West and acted as they were told. Thus they refused to even discuss the proposal of a new constitution for Germany which had been put forward by the 'Central Round Table'; they did not examine in detail the 1000-page treaty that was to be the basis for unification; and they agreed the dogma of privatisation and the early introduction of the West German currency.

So why did so many GDR citizens vote for the CDU and a hasty unification? Many undoubtedly thought that unification would allow them to keep all the positive aspects that pertained in the GDR (women's rights, educational opportunity, job security, cheap housing, good welfare support and a subsidised culture), but at the same time give them the opportunity of enjoying the much more extensive material wealth the West Germans had and to take advantage of the world travel opportunities that the German Mark would also bring with it.

Currency union

On 1 July 1990, even before formal unification between the GDR and the FRG had taken place, a hasty currency union was pushed through, with the result that the GDR economy was plunged into bankruptcy. Before unification the West German Mark was valued at around 4.5 GDR Marks. However, at currency union the GDR Mark was fixed at parity with the West German Mark at a rate of 1:1 with the result that GDR export products rose in price by 400-500 per cent overnight, and were therefore no longer competitive; the export market (39 per cent of the GDR economy) inevitably collapsed. In addition, the GDR market was, literally overnight, flooded by West German products, which also severely damaged the internal market.

Much was made subsequently of the 'collapse of the out-dated and rotten GDR industries'. What was not explained was that the collapse was directly related to the hasty introduction of the new currency without any transition period.[60]

Karl Pöhl, president of the Bundesbank, (the German federal or central bank) from 1980 to 1991, in a perhaps unguarded comment, said that the GDR had been completely unprepared for monetary union with West Germany and the result had been 'a catastrophe'. Kohl was furious with the messenger, as Dan van der Vat pointed out in his obituary of Pöhl. According to Karl Schachtschneider, professor emeritus in public and civil law:

> The revaluation of the GDR's currency by around 500 per cent took away any chance of them keeping their own markets, both at home and abroad, so that a restructuring of the GDR economy by its own efforts was rendered nigh impossible. The currency change-over was … a crass injustice and represented a serious infraction of basic economic legality, which essentially should be duty bound to protect working people, above all to allow them the opportunity of supporting themselves through their own efforts.[61]

Rainer Gohlke, the former director of German Railways and short-term boss of the Treuhand, told the Bundestag's investigative committee into the Treuhand, during a public hearing, that 'a revaluation of a currency by 400-500 per cent would have a dramatic influence on any country's economy, but particularly one reliant on exports. He went on to say that a country could cope with a revaluation of perhaps four to five per cent by increasing production, 'but anything above that would mean bankruptcy'.[62]

Before that same committee, Jochen Homann, Minister for business and technology, said that the collapse of the

GDR economy was 'in principle the direct result' of a lack of 'protection from outside'; 'it was a crash course that had immediate consequences!'[63] When asked how he would summarise the status of the GDR economy within Europe, Gohlke answered, 'The GDR was among the strongest economies in the Eastern bloc. It was in fact the foremost. If one looks at its gross domestic product in comparison with other European Community countries, than it was not at the bottom of the list.' He went on to explain that GDR products had a high reputation in the Eastern bloc, but also that many GDR products were sold in the old Federal Republic, 'formerly we imported products from the East on an ongoing basis, furniture etc. All of a sudden that collapsed and no one, not even us, bought these products anymore'.

The sudden imposition of the Deutsch Mark without any transition period, was a political, rather than an economic decision. Chancellor Kohl had been warned by his Finance Minister and financial experts of the probable consequences of such a hurried introduction and they had recommended a staged process; but Kohl and his party wanted full unity as soon as possible so that they could claim all the credit. 1990 was, after all, an election year in West Germany.

The Treuhand and the asset-stripping process

After the fall of the Wall, the new government, faced with increasing pressure for the unification of the two Germanies, was increasingly concerned about what would happen to the GDR's assets which belonged to the people (Volkseigentum). It therefore passed legislation, on 15 March 1990, to set up a Trusteeship quango (Treuhandanstalt) to ensure the rights and property of the citizens. 'Treuhand' literally translated means loyal hand or trustee i.e. an individual or institution entrusted to look after and administer certain interests on behalf of someone else. The government passed this legislation in an attempt to protect what was rightfully the people's property from vulture capitalists. In the GDR the vast number of businesses were publicly-owned enterprises (VEBs) i.e. run by the state on behalf of the people who were the genuine owners.

The country had more than 12,000 such enterprises with four million employees. At unification, its industrial assets were estimated, by West German experts, at around 650 billion Deutsch Marks which meant that every citizen 'owned' assets to the value of around 40,000 Deutsch Marks each.[64] The Treuhand as envisaged by the Modrow government was to be tasked with ensuring that GDR citizens received certificates of ownership which could later be exchanged, not for cash, but to obtain housing, business premises or similar assets. The setting up of the Treuhand was also intended to ensure that 'publicly-owned enterprises' would not be treated like 'state-owned assets'. This had been one of the demands made by those who took to the streets in 1989 before the Wall came down, shouting: 'We are the people'. If this measure were not carried out, it would be clear, that the people would be 'expropriated'.

This was important because of the real capital wealth created by workers in the GDR, of which 80 per cent was incorporated into publicly-owned assets, while only 20 per cent was actually owned by individual citizens; in the Federal Republic proportional ownership relationships were the reverse. Even then Finance Minister, Theo Waigel, conceded on 7 February 1990 in the West German parliament that the issuing of people's shares in order to distribute the publicly owned assets in East Germany should be considered.[65]

The 1990 elections were characterised as the GDR's 'first free elections' – and certainly elections in GDR times had not been genuinely democratic. However, although the GDR was still a sovereign state and the Modrow government of national responsibility had agreed that no Federal German politicians should interfere in the upcoming elections, there was heavy interference by West Germany, with large sums of money donated, the printing of election propaganda and the free service of 'advisers' from West Germany's big political parties.[66]

The GDR elections on 18 March 1990 changed everything. A conservative government was elected which took its cue from the Kohl government and pressed for a speedy unification. After those elections, the idea of 'publicly owned' assets being transferred to the citizens by the Treuhand was quietly dropped during this short-lived interim government, in blatant contravention of the statutory legislation passed by the previous GDR parliament, with no consultation or referendum taking place. No certificates of ownership were issued to the people and they received no compensation whatsoever.

The mandate of the Treuhand was changed and the emphasis was now placed on a speedy privatisation of all enterprises, which meant expropriation of all assets owned collectively by GDR citizens. This action signified a double constitutional violation. It was a violation of the GDR's own constitution, still in force at the time and valid until unification in October 1990. According to Article 10 of that constitution all publicly-owned property was to be given protection, and Article 16 stated that 'Expropriation would take place only in cases where general social benefit could be demonstrated and only in accordance with proper legal procedure and on the basis of appropriate compensation'. It also signified a violation of the German Federal Republic's own constitution, which states that: 'an expropriation is only permissible in cases where there is general social benefit' ... 'and it can only be undertaken in accordance with a law stipulating the means and extent of that expropriation as well as the payment of due compensation.'

On 31 July 1990, at a press conference, the new head of the Treuhand, Rainer Gohlke, a West German appointee, set out its aim as follows: 'Our aim is to secure as many jobs as possible, make as many companies as possible competitive. And those that stand no chance will be restructured as quickly as possible or, as appropriate, closed'.[67] Gohlke did not last long, within just a few weeks he was replaced by Detlev Rohwedder who changed the emphasis from restructuring and rebuilding to privatisation as the only way forward. What followed was the largest and most rapid privatisation ever seen in any country in the world (except perhaps in the Soviet Union under Yeltsin). Never in the history of civilisation has a state's total assets and infrastructure been disposed of so rapidly and in such a criminal fashion. Its machinations make Al Capone look like a paragon of capitalist virtue.

Handing the Treuhand over to West German appointees was seen as a green light to sell off all the GDR's publicly-owned enterprises at breakneck speed and at knockdown prices – some factories which were perfectly viable were sold for as little as 1 Deutsch Mark. There was only a pretence at proper tendering or of attempting to find the highest bids and some of the privatisation process even involved criminal methods and a misuse of state subsidies. The Treuhand managed to convert GDR assets valued at over 650 billion Deutsch Marks into a debt mountain of 260 billion Deutsch Marks. In other words within four years of Treuhand operations 860 billion Deutsch Marks were spent on privatising and destroying GDR industry.

Even if not admitted publicly, the Treuhand, once in Western hands, saw its task as overseeing the rapid dismantling of GDR state assets so that no potential competition with West German companies would arise. This was legitimised by the allegation that GDR industry was 'marode' i.e. rotten, and could not be rescued anyway. Apart from the fact that UN statistics contradict that claim.[68] During the 1980s, the GDR had bought over 700 top-of-the-range industrial complexes to help modernise some of its key industries. These are still productive today and are bringing in profits for their new owners – so a description of the whole GDR economy as 'rotten' is hardly accurate.

The Treuhand set about eradicating any legacy of GDR socialism with alacrity: 3,400 factories, 520 large construction companies, 465 state farms[69] and thousands of other smaller companies were privatised, and soon thereafter many were closed. In the countryside 1.7 million hectares of agricultural and forest land were sold off. Privatisation (in reality straightforward asset-stripping) was seen as an ideological imperative. And all this took place within only four years.

A few 'cherries', though, were successfully privatised and kept going; they have since brought their new owners big profits: the Zeiss optical instrument factory in Jena, the largest East German steel works (EKO) and most of the Baltic ship yards. They became successful enterprises, albeit with severely reduced staffing levels – Zeiss, for instance, had 20,000 employees in GDR times but today a mere 2,000.

As an interesting aside, the last historical incidence of the German government setting up a 'Treuhand' institution had been when the Nazis used it to expropriate Jewish and Polish properties and 'legalise' their transference to new 'Aryan' owners.

Once the GDR companies had been taken into administration by the Treuhand, their managers were sacked and West German managers, some emerging from retirement for that purpose, were called in to run them, even some who had been forcibly retired as a result of incompetence[70]. Gerhard Friedrich, a CDU member of the Bundestag investigative committee looking at Treuhand practices, mentioned in a meeting that as a practising lawyer himself he 'noticed that all my seemingly unsuccessful colleagues were suddenly to be found over there [i.e. in East Germany]. They were all trying to do deals and the Treuhand's statutory obligations were constantly flouted.'[71]

One surprising revelation came from Manfred Balz, the former legal director of the Treuhand. He told the same Bundestag investigative committee, sarcastically, that Rohwedder's refusal to transform GDR enterprises into public shareholding companies was 'heilsamer Ungehorsam' (healthy disregard of regulations) in terms of his legal obligations. Otto Schily, Minister of the Interior, suggested that this 'healthy disregard of regulations and was nothing less than arbitrary decision-making and a flouting of the legal process.' Balz did not deny this.

In the aftermath of the rapid privatisation of GDR assets by the Treuhand, it became increasingly clear that the whole process had been deeply flawed, and was characterised by unaccountable, incompetent and even criminal action. The process had also been facilitated by the use of fear tactics to intimidate and cow GDR citizens and feed the media juicy scare stories, which certainly helped to hinder any protests about what was happening. The witch hunt against former Stasi informants and those deemed to have been close collaborators with the state was an ideal tool too. For instance the popular tabloid *Bild* newspaper ran the scary headline: 'Putch! Stasi is handing out guns!' in its 22 January edition. This story was pure fabrication.

Former GDR Secretary of State with responsibility for foreign trade, Gerhard Beil, writes in his memoirs that immediately after unification around, 'one hundred thousand investigations, interrogations and house searches were undertaken [by government authorities] and these created an atmosphere of fear, insecurity and suspicion. They were at the same time a smokescreen for the inconspicuous takeover of the banks, insurance and trading organisations in the GDR. All that was to deflect attention from the billions of Marks-worth of assets that were rapidly disposed of.[72]

The questionable and sometimes corrupt way in which the Treuhand disposed of GDR assets was documented by *Spiegel* reporter Dieter Kampe in his book about the Treuhand.[73] He examined in great detail what went on behind the deals that were made by 'this super bureaucracy, the Treuhand'. He reconstructs some of the spectacular scandals that took place during the sale of enterprises and 'the often dubious interests involved in the Treuhand's disposal of the people's assets ... from downright incompetent decision-making to the toleration of criminal activity. He gives the unbelievable example of the way the Geräte- und Regelwerke Teltow, near Berlin, was sold. This was one of the country's biggest manufacturers of electrical equipment. It had over 12,000 employees. A Frankfurt businessman, Claus Wisser, was able to purchase it for 1 Deutsch Mark, after giving assurances on job security and future investment which, however, were not enforceable or legally binding.

The company had been independently valued at between 170-270 million Deutsch Marks. In the end, Kampe drew the conclusion that a rapid privatisation took precedence over everything else, with the result that this public institution became a 'help-yourself shop for dubious investors'. His well-evidenced critique runs like a red thread through the book.

What follows are a few prominent examples of how GDR industry was dismantled.

Interflug airline
The privatisation of the GDR airline company Interflug was a particularly crass case. It was a profitable and successful business with a good safety record and high standing. Only a few years before unification, it had

purchased three new airbuses to update its fleet. There were several interested bidders, including Lufthansa, Aer Lingus, British Airways and Cathay Pacific. Potential foreign investors were deterred and experts in the field felt that a merger between Lufthansa and Interflug would be the most sensible option. However Lufthansa saw its East German counterpart merely as a potential competitor, so wanted it closed down. The same applied to the airport at Schönefeld which would have become a potentially keen competitor with West Berlin's airport in Tegel. Foreign investors were again deterred by press assertions that the GDR had no properly trained technicians to service the airbuses, and it would therefore not be safe to fly in them. Interflug was closed down.

Mysteriously, the papers relating to the eventual disposal of the company have gone missing, so any proper investigation is no longer possible. Robert Ide, an editor with the German newspaper, *Tagesspiegel*, wrote that 'The demise of the state airline company concluded a financial crime story, which today stands as an example for the restoration/clean-up policy of the Treuhand'.[74]

Shipbuilding

This industry in the GDR had been very successful. After the Second World War, there was virtually no shipbuilding at all on East Germany's coast, but over the years shipyards were built in Rostock, Wismar, Warnemünde, Stralsund and other cities. By 1990, over 5,000 sea-going and internal waterway boats of 200 different types had been built. To give some indication of the quality of these, Lloyds Shipping Register noted that GDR-built ships for the fishing industry were top of the list, and cargo ships took second or third place in terms of world shipbuilding figures – and this data was not culled from SED propaganda publications but calculated by experts in the business.

In the formerly mainly agricultural region of

Mecklenburg, shipbuilding became the biggest employer providing around 56,000 jobs at its height. By 1989, the shipyards had supplied more than 3,500 ships to the Soviet Union alone. Within two years, after unification, the shipyards, now owned by a West German company, had cut the number of jobs to 13,500. Today there is only a skeleton boat-building operation remaining in the whole territory of the former GDR.

Merchant navy

The extensive GDR merchant marine fleet was also broken up, sold off and its crews sacked. This is a prime example that can be cited to refute the allegation that the GDR's economic infrastructure was, as a whole, rotten and unsalvageable. Its merchant fleet alone would have been accepted throughout the world as ample evidence of the country's credit worthiness. It was set up in 1950 and by 1977 it had 203 cargo ships sailing 28 lines. Within 25 years it had become one of Europe's biggest fleets, with 11,000 employees.

The West German shipping companies demanded the scrapping of the GDR's fleet to get rid of competition – they already had over-capacity. Eight prospective purchasers were interested in the fleet, but in the end it was sold to a medium-sized consortium set up by the investment company Rah Schües from Hamburg, which immediately proceeded to break it up.

VEB Scharfenstein

The VEB Scharfenstein refrigerator company, with four production units in the GDR, produced household refrigerators not only for the home market but had export partners in 30 countries. Just prior to unification it was producing over a million fridges and freezer units per year. After unification the Treuhand took it over.

It originally had 5,500 employees, but three years after

the Treuhand took over only 630 of those were still employed by the company. Everyone in the factory feared for their jobs because even though it had been the biggest manufacturer of refrigerators in the Eastern bloc, by 1992 it was facing bankruptcy. In an attempt to save jobs and give the company a new lease of life, one of the company's engineers, Albrecht Meyer, together with the West German environmentalist, Wolfgang Lohbeck, made a technological breakthrough, enabling the company to manufacture more environmentally-friendly refrigerators.

In their research and development the company collaborated with Greenpeace and the Dortmund Hygiene Institute to develop the world's first refrigerator free of chlorofluorocarbon and hydrofluorocarbon. Instead of using chemicals that damage the ozone layer, the new units used gases like propane and butane for cooling. The company was renamed 'Foron' and went on to produce 650 million of the new units after its reorganisation.

This innovation represented a serious threat to the market dominance of traditional refrigerator manufacturers in the West. They immediately countered with a massive and disingenuous propaganda campaign condemning the new design fallaciously as dangerous and environmentally unfriendly.

This campaign succeeded in ruining Foron's reputation – the political climate made it easy to deprecate an East German product. Foron was forced out of the market and in 1996 it went bankrupt and was taken over by a Dutch company.

On the insistence of Greenpeace, the new technology developed by Foron had not been patented because Greenpeace wanted it to be adopted quickly by other manufacturers. When those other companies did eventually begin manufacturing similar ones they could make free use of Foron's technology without having to buy any patents. That was an additional bitter pill. In the meantime, most manufacturers have taken on the technology developed by Foron and it has now become a standard for the environmentally-friendly manufacture of refrigerators worldwide.

VEB Nähmaschinenwerk

The VEB Nähmaschinenwerk (the former pre-war Singer-owned sewing machine factory) in Wittenberge had become one of the world's leading manufacturers and the leading company for the production and sale of sewing machines in central and western Europe. It also had one of the most modern foundries in Europe.

The Treuhand sold it to the Indonesian HAS Group through the agency of Joergen Knoop-Schade resident in Hamburg. The purchasing company promised to invest 60 million Deutsch Marks and guarantee job security for the 800 employees until 1994 and maintain continued production until 1996 – but on condition that 40,000 household sewing machines were produced and exported to Indonesia during the year of 'purchase' (1991). Under stressful and intensive work conditions, massive overtime and reduced wages, the promised machines were produced and transported to Indonesia. Once the containers with the sewing machines arrived in Indonesia the company lost interest in the Wittenberge factory. By 2008 Knoop-Schade was in prison convicted of carrying out a murder contract. The nominal owner of the Indonesian company had vanished. As rapidly as the sewing machines disappeared in Indonesia, the Treuhand managed to make the East German factory disappear. The man responsible for such operations wrote to the factory on 23 October 1991 stating that the sewing machine factory in Wittenberge was 'not salvageable' and was to be closed down. By 2001, the brand logo was deleted from the patent and business brand registry and the land on which the factory stood is now owned by a bank.

Although the management and employees of GDR companies were taken totally by surprise when their factories were closed down and/or sold off, there were numerous examples of occupations, strikes and legal challenges by employees, as well as a number of attempts by management and workers to take over the managing of their own factories, but none of these efforts was successful. The rapidity of the whole process left them completely stranded.

One prominent example where the workers took year-long strike action was the potash mining company (Kaliwerk) in Bischofferode, Thuringia, with the evocative name of Thomas Müntzer. It was the biggest employer in the region, with over 1,000 employees and had a long tradition. Around 90 per cent of its potash was exported to western Europe. When the Treuhand announced its decision in 1990 to close it down, the workers began a long, determined and high-profile struggle to keep it open, even undertaking a two-week march to Berlin and going on hunger strike. In April 1993, 500 of the workers occupied the mine, organising a work-in. It became a beacon for resistance in East Germany to the deliberate and wanton destruction of the economic infrastructure. In the end, though, it was sold to the West German competitor company, Mitteldeutsche Kali AG, based in Kassel, which then promptly closed it in December 1993.

These few examples can be replicated time and time again, and serve to demonstrate that the Treuhand's role was, in essence, to asset-strip the GDR as fast as possible, even at the cost of circumventing legal norms and turning a blind eye to criminality. The result has seen a de-industrialisation of a once prosperous region. The number of jobs in industrial manufacturing fell by 75 per cent. As a result, young people were forced to move West in their search for work.

The deplorable balance sheet of the Treuhand's business

activities will remain largely veiled or will be denied and its criminal raiding activities will never be fully exposed. That is as true for its methodology as for the enormous sums of money that were allegedly spent on 'saving' the East German economy but in reality disappeared in the accounts of its West German competitors or in those of letter box companies whose real owners have never been traced. Even politicians known for their anti-GDR attitudes only rarely attempt to deny these facts. And more evidence of this criminality came from a surprising quarter: Two of the lawyers employed by the BvS (Bundesanstalt für vereinigungsbedingte Sonderaufgaben, which is the successor institution to the Treuhand), Kai Renken and Werner Jenke, wrote a report on 'Financial criminality during the unification process' which concluded that 'at the very latest with the fall of the Wall on 9 November 1989, there began not only a rapid process of re-unification of both German states but also a collapse of state authority in the GDR, making possible a very particular form of economic criminality, a so-called unification criminality, representing a not very glorious chapter in the German unification process'.[75]

What in essence happened under the Treuhand was a complete transfer without compensation of property and assets accumulated over forty years through hard work and effort by GDR citizens, as well as the land they owned (which in the GDR had no monetary value as such) to, in the main, West German owners. This transfer of a country's assets – unprecedented anywhere in the world during peacetime – amounted to billions of Euros: a robbing of ordinary people for the enrichment of a few. Of those companies and individuals who bought GDR property, 80 per cent were West Germans, only 10 per cent were from other countries and a mere 5 per cent went to GDR citizens.

Even the land reform which had been carried out under the Potsdam Agreement after the war was in effect reversed by the new German government. Former large landowners were able to buy back their former estates for 40 per cent of the market price.

As a result of the destruction of the GDR's economic base, according to a social survey carried out in 2007, the population on former GDR territory was, at this time, made up of 43 per cent pensioners – the young had been forced to migrate to find jobs – and 4 out of 10 were officially deemed to be living in 'economically precarious circumstances'.[76] That situation was particularly evident in rural areas and small towns where newcomers from other regions or EU countries were less likely to settle. After the collapse of the GDR and unification two million citizens left the territory, above all young people.

The so-called old debts

East German private households had virtually no debt. People spent what they had and no more – there was no tradition of buying on tick. The overwhelming majority of GDR citizens had no loans and hire purchase did not exist. However, most publicly-owned enterprises, co-operatives and local authorities entered life under the new economic system after the demise of the GDR burdened with oppressively high 'old debt'.

How did these 'old debts' come about? In accordance with the GDR's economic system, all publicly-owned enterprises paid almost their total profits to the central GDR state bank. The bank then returned to the enterprises credit for investment and general running costs. In addition, the national planning commission set targets for production levels and granted appropriate credits to realise them. Local authorities were tasked with building a certain number of homes for which they also received funding. In other words, these credits were not loans as in a Western market economy because they were not initiated by the 'borrowers'. There was no formal creditor and debtor because all parties were an integral part of the centrally planned economy and operated with funds from the same public purse.

Shortly after the introduction of the West German currency on 1 July 1990 (i.e. three months before unification), West German banks were allowed to buy the (state-owned) GDR banks at a cost well below their actual value. Suddenly, all credits that had been provided by the GDR government to enterprises or local authorities were now counted as debts to the banks on West German terms and a high interest rate was slapped on them. In this way the West German banks took on the 'debts' to the tune of 180 billion Deutsch Marks - money which they had never lent in the first place. The original loans had been agreed with the GDR state bank at an interest rate of 0.5 per cent. However, the new West German owners promptly and unilaterally increased the interest rate to the then market rate of 10 per cent. This offered a lucrative income for the banks but it spelt disaster for the many factories, cooperatives and local authorities who were, all of a sudden, not only considered to have debts but also faced huge interest payments.

As a result, many enterprises that would normally have survived even in the new market economy became unviable overnight because of the debt burden. And others were sold off at a fraction of their value because of their 'old debts'. Many cooperatives were forced to dissolve and the communities are still struggling under the burden of debts they have to pay, even on blocks of flats that are being or have been pulled down because people, particularly the young, have moved to the West in their hunt for work.

A number of legal challenges were mounted, but the German Supreme Court handed down a ruling that these 'old' debts and their transfer to West German private banks were perfectly legal. Karl Albrecht Schachtschneider, professor of public law at the University of Nürnberg-Erlangen, in western Germany, was so concerned about the apparent unfairness of the 'old debts' that he decided to take the case to the Constitutional Court. He wrote a book about the nature of the debts setting out his reasoning as to why he believed the so-called 'old debts' were a fabrication and an injustice to the people and communities of the GDR.[77] However, after three years of deliberation, the Constitutional Court dismissed the case.

The decapitation of the GDR's intellectual workforce

The unification process, which in practice amounted to an annexation of the GDR, had all the hallmarks of a colonisation. The intellectual elite was stigmatised, marginalised and dismissed, so that it could be replaced by personnel from Western Germany.

The form this process would take was laid down in the unification treaty, a 1000-page document that was, to a large extent, elaborated by the Federal Republic and simply nodded through by the last GDR parliament without proper examination. The treaty basically defined three ways of marginalising the GDR's intellectual sector: the closing down of research centres, the introduction of evaluation assessments for academics and political vetting.

Among the institutions that were to be closed were prestigious intellectual centres like the GDR's Academy of Sciences and the Academy of Arts. In order to illustrate the enormity of that decision, it is perhaps of interest to know that the Academy of Sciences had 55 research institutes that included mathematics, all the natural sciences, medicine as well as social science, the humanities and arts with well over 20,000 staff. In addition, whole institutions with an emphasis on social science and a range of departments at universities and higher education colleges were also marked down for closure. These included institutes and departments dealing with economics, history, the law, philosophy, pedagogy, psychology and sport – but also specialist centres like the Institute for Latin American studies and the Institute for Disaster and Emergency Medicine in Rostock.

The idea was to demonstrate to the general public that a cleansing process was taking place. The result of which was that thousands of lecturers and researchers were purged. They not only lost their tenured jobs but were also stripped of their legal contracts and seniority protections.

Those who did manage to hold on to their jobs were subjected to a vetting process in which so-called evaluating commissions (staffed only by West German academics) assessed the professional competence and personal integrity of all academics. The reason given for the necessity of this vetting was the alleged low academic standard of research in the GDR, i.e. the assumption that it was all manipulated to serve the ideological demands of the regime.

The assessments were, it seemed, an attempt to denigrate East German intellectual achievement and to break up key centres of research. The process was demeaning and humiliating, and a number of internationally renowned academics refused to undergo it and so were dismissed on the spot.

During this process those academics and researchers not immediately sacked were placed 'on hold' (Warteschleife). This also meant that they lost their employment rights and could easily be dismissed once the 'holding period' came to an end.

The actual result of the evaluation surprised the assessors themselves since they had to admit that the standards were, despite often inferior material conditions, comparable to those in the West. Yet it was too late, the assumption of an 'academic desert' or, more to the point, the imposition of an ideologically-determined plan to oust the GDR intellectual elite, had led to the decision to close down these centres of research. Academics and researchers were, overnight, obliged to go job hunting which, in most cases, took place on an individual basis so that research teams, especially in medicine and the natural sciences, were torn apart.

About half the GDR's 14,000 scientists and researchers had worked in research and development in the large enterprises that all had their own R&D departments. With the destruction of industry or the radical down-sizing of even very successful firms to become mere branch workshops for Western companies, research in industry was reduced by 50 per cent within a year of unification and today R&D is hardly carried out at all on the territory of the former GDR.

The most glaring example of this was at the Carl Zeiss Jena complex, one of the world leaders in the development and production of precision optics. Zeiss had produced lenses for the space industry and for other demanding optical purposes. After unification it was taken over by its competitor company in the West, its workforce was reduced and today there is no more R&D.

The third method of cleansing the intellectual elite was the political vetting of every employee in education (schools, colleges and universities). All staff had to complete questionnaires that, in addition to professional qualifications, asked for detailed information on their present and former party affiliations, political opinions and activities. Although such questions are illegal under the German constitution, people from the GDR were told that the completion of the questionnaires was a pre-condition of further employment.

Teachers were found politically unacceptable on the basis of trivial activities, such as being a choir leader, because this was considered to be an activity supportive of the system. The arbitrariness of this political vetting was glaring: thus in Thuringia (governed by the Christian Democratic Party) every ninth teacher was found politically suspect, whereas in Brandenburg (governed by the Social Democrats) only one in 34 was.

As a result of the information given in the questionnaires (or as a result of individuals refusing to fill them in) 75,000 teachers lost their jobs and were blacklisted on the basis of their former political activities or associations. This seemed a convenient way of reducing the number of teachers since class sizes in GDR schools were smaller than in the Federal Republic, and in universities, the ratio of lecturer to student was 1:5 whereas in the Federal Republic it is 1:18.

The closing down of academic institutions and university departments as well as political vetting resulted in more than one million people with a university degree or its equivalent losing their jobs. This constituted 50 per cent of that group and it meant that, percentage-wise, the Eastern part of Germany, following unification, had the highest unemployment rate for university graduates in the world. The number of those involved in university teaching and research was reduced to a third. Leading scientists were forced to go abroad or had to accept fixed-term contracts, and not a small number was forced to take early retirement. All university chancellors, directors of state enterprises, research institutes and even museums lost their jobs and many were blacklisted.

All in all, 78 research and associated institutes were closed down. The result was a complete destruction of the GDR's scientific research potential, a terrible intellectual haemorrhage from universities and colleges – in essence a complete eradication of 40 years' accumulated experience and history of the GDR by marginalising those who were best placed to pass that knowledge on to future generations.

GDR state television and radio were also closed down a year after unification and the vast majority of employees sacked. The new regional television and radio stations that were set up afterwards employed almost exclusively West

Germans and only a handful of journalists from the former GDR were taken on. Of the 78 publishing houses that existed in the GDR, only 12 remain although several new ones were founded. An enormous reservoir of expertise was lost.

In this context, it is perhaps of interest to note the comments made by Dr. Ingeborg Syllm-Rapoport when she was granted her doctorate in Hamburg over 70 years after completing her studies, at the age of 102. Her case made headlines in Germany. She had completed her medical studies in Germany during the 1930s, but was denied her doctorate when the Nazis came to power. Being an active communist and Jewish, she was forced to flee the country and found exile in the USA. But with the rise of McCarthyism in the post-war period she and her husband, also a doctor, were summoned to appear before the House Committee on Un-American Activities. Persecution once again forced them to leave the country and they eventually settled in the GDR.

Happy as she was to receive her degree belatedly in 2015, she said that the preparations recalled enough bad memories to rob her of sleep – of brown-shirted Nazis shouting and stamping at lectures by professors classified as Jews, but also of the years after the end of the GDR in 1989. 'I would never have believed, more than 45 years after the victory over Hitler fascism and 40 years after the McCarthy era, that I would again experience such a flood of sackings, such mass destruction of livelihoods and contempt for talents', she said.

Housing vultures

After unification, hundreds of thousands of East Germans suddenly found that the security they enjoyed in the homes they had bought or rented was suddenly threatened.

When the unification treaty was being negotiated, the West German government had insisted on the principle of 'restitution before compensation' for properties in the East that once belonged to those who had left East Germany permanently.

As a consequence, any post-war property transactions that had taken place within the territory of East Germany were deemed questionable. This gave previous owners, who had left immediately after the war or during the early years of the GDR, the right to reclaim these properties with no obligation to pay any compensation whatsoever. This meant that those who had bought these homes and often improved them over a period of 40 years, were suddenly threatened with eviction. The former owners, who had already received compensation in the West for their loss of property, were now given the right to reclaim them as well. Of course, in the meantime, the value of these properties had increased massively, especially in and around Berlin where the increase was up to a hundredfold. This fact alone attracted huge numbers of claimants.

In fact, 2.2 million requests were lodged for legal re-possession of houses and blocks of flats. Because several people usually live in a single home, it meant that about half the GDR population was affected by such claims. Demands were made not just with respect to single homes and blocks of flats, but whole streets and even villages.

Overnight, many GDR families found themselves evicted from homes they had bought or leased and had considered their own; a number even committed suicide as a result. Others, at considerable cost, were forced to fight through the courts in an attempt to keep their homes. Many, who had rented their flats from the local authority over many years suddenly found themselves with a private landlord who invariably tried to have them evicted so that they could bring in new tenants and increase the rent.

Yet of all the claimants, only three per cent were in fact

former owners, the others were merely relatives of former owners, often with conflicting interests, sometimes relatives who had never even lived in Germany and did not speak the language. But they all suddenly found themselves with an unexpected windfall, an opportunity to own property.

What followed was a period of fear and grinding uncertainty for the current owners and long drawn-out battles with relatives of the previous owners, the administrative authorities and the courts. These battles took years and during that time the current owners were in limbo, not allowed to undertake any repairs, obtain loans or sell the properties. In the end, after often strenuous and expensive legal battles which often dragged on for years, 60 per cent of claims were rejected. That in itself demonstrates the greed of those who were out to make a fortune on the backs of the East Germans. By 2007, almost half a million properties had been handed back to (relatives of) former owners and the current owners were forced out.

It would have been much better if previous owners had been given compensation, as happened after the war, as that would have precluded claims on the actual properties as well. That would have provided for peace and stability. But keeping half of the GDR population in continuous fear over the possible loss of their homes was, it seems, a more attractive alternative. People who live in fear do not protest or challenge what else is happening around them.

Evidence that the decision to permit restitution before compensation was a political one and not based on the basic principles of property ownership is the fact that any claims of restitution by East Germans for properties they lost in the West through the partition of Germany were rejected on the grounds that the time limits for bringing such claims had expired.

Women – the biggest losers

Women in the GDR were the largest group to lose out through unification. They may now have access to material goods not available before, but they have been pushed back into dependence by a dominant ideology of women serving men. In the GDR, 88 per cent of all adult women worked and another 8.5 per cent were in full-time education, which meant that 96.5 per cent took an active part in the wider social context outside the home and they also had their own income.

Work was the basis for economic independence, a sense of self-worth, a place for communication and social interaction, not just a source for additional household income or, as some critics have argued, a state-imposed, obligatory activity.

Women were highly skilled – only 6 per cent had no qualification at all, as against 24 per cent of West German working women. In the GDR, 50 per cent of all jobs in medicine and law were carried out by women and a third of women worked in technical professions. Given the great importance that work represented to women in terms of their identity, unemployment on the scale that happened after unification had a devastating effect. Even after 20 years, on the territory of the former GDR, two thirds of the unemployed were women (in agriculture it was as much as 75 per cent) and they made up at least 70 per cent of the long-term unemployed.

Post-unification, the labour market was biased against women; men had a better chance of finding alternative work. For women over 50 it was especially difficult, and many suddenly found themselves unemployable. Women doctors over 40, who lost their jobs when the health centres – the typical form of health provision in the GDR – were closed found it difficult to set up their own practices –

the typical form of health provision in the Federal Republic.

Women academics too found themselves in a very difficult situation. In the highly competitive job market, where academics are chasing diminishing funds, a predictable hierarchy operates: first West German men, second East German men, third West German women, fourth East German women.

Although gender discrimination was by no means completely abolished in the GDR, this blatant disparaging of women as a group appeared like history going into reverse. This perception is underlined by the fact that, in the general hunt for jobs, children are now deemed to represent a problem. It is well-known that the GDR had excellent childcare facilities which made it possible to combine work and parenthood without financial hardship. In 1989, 68 per cent of working women in the GDR had children under the age of 18, whereas in the Federal Republic it was only 25 per cent.

Not only was the number of working women with children much lower in the West, there was a tendency to create a divide between career women without children (usually professionals) and working women with children, often only in part-time work.

The increased private responsibility for childcare combined with the anxiety over job prospects for both men and women has led to the shifting of the burden of once accepted equal responsibilities back onto women. A common formulation used by the media is 'men become unemployed, women become housewives'. GDR women witnessed a bizarre new campaign to promote the role of the housewife. Many women found this amusing, but also insulting, because it indicated that they might have to fight, once again, the battles their grandmothers fought and won.

Unification brought another considerable change for women: the abolition of their right to an abortion on demand. In the GDR, since 1972, women had had the legal right to terminate their pregnancy free of charge within the first 12 weeks. West Germany has a penal code (paragraph 218) which states that abortion is unlawful and those who attempt to abort face up to three years in prison or a fine.

After unification it became necessary to bring West German and East German law on this issue into alignment. In 1992, paragraph 218 was amended to adopt GDR legislation, but a compulsory consultation prior to the procedure was added.

After protests from the CDU/CSU and the Bavarian state government, which wanted abortion itself to remain illegal, even this amendment was declared null and void by Germany's Constitutional Court only one year later. The law was reworked with the result that today abortion remains generally unlawful but not punishable if a pregnant woman can demonstrate to the doctor that she has undergone consultation prior to requesting an abortion.

Even 20 years after unification there still exists a very different perception of equal rights among women in the territory of the former GDR. According to an investigation undertaken in 2008, 80 per cent of East German women wanted an equal division of labour in the family, but only 50 per cent of West German women, among whom traditional family models still exerted a strong force. In fact, the more emancipated consciousness of GDR women has increasingly influenced women in the West, even though sociologists appear to be unaware of where this new confidence has come from.[78]

East Germans treated worse than the Nazis

Hitler's fascist Germany, based as it was on an ideology of virulent racism, led to the deaths of millions of people. The GDR state and society was based on an ethical idea aimed at creating a society based on solidarity, cooperation, peace with other nations and socialism. Even if these efforts resulted in the establishment of authoritarian structures, the contrast with fascism could not be greater. This, however, has not prevented the powers that be in the West from conflating the two systems under the banner of totalitarianism and in fact using the GDR as the scapegoat for all the evils perpetrated during Germany's turbulent 20th century.

Although GDR citizens in their majority voted for unification in spring 1990, few would have been aware that there was a sting in the tail of the new German beast. Many have been treated more like the proverbial stepchildren in a Grimm's fairy tale than true 'brothers and sisters' by the government of the new and enlarged Germany. Why was that?

In its treatment of the GDR and those who were deemed to have been active upholders of the system, the authorities in the Federal Republic argue that they do not wish to miss the opportunity 'this time' of dealing properly with the legacy of a second totalitarian system to have befallen the German nation during the twentieth century. With this official policy, German fascism and communism have been put in the same pot, but this convenient recipe of confusion conceals a dark reality.

One could argue that the way the GDR and its legacy has been, and still is being, treated is a logical continuation of the animosity towards socialist ideas that has its roots in the anti-socialist laws brought in by Bismarck as far back as 1878. This process continued through to the support given by big business interests and a conservative academia to Hitler's Nazis in their attempt 'to stem the tide of Bolshevism,' to the banning of the German Communist Party (KPD) and the blacklisting of communists or close sympathisers in the Federal Republic from the 1950s onwards.[79] After the KPD was banned, there were over 500,000 judicial investigations into individuals suspected of communist activities and at least 10,000 convictions, including prison sentences, were handed down against communists, trade unionists, pacifists and other leftists.[80]

While West Germany after the war took on all the trappings of a mainstream western democracy, it still contained within its constitution, its structures and the practices of its legal system elements of a Nazi juridical and ideological legacy, and never fully carried out a thorough de-nazification of society. This process was given support by the western occupying powers. Once the Nuremberg trials were over and the Cold War had set in, the enemy was once again communism and the Soviet Union. Ex-Nazis were, of course, very useful to the western allies in that battle and were duly enlisted. A continued investigation into Nazi crimes and the judicial pursuance of Nazi criminals was suppressed. And because so many former Nazi officials were soon back in their old jobs, including many lawyers and civil servants, they were more than willing to continue harassing communists and left-wingers and to protect their former Nazi colleagues.

The treatment of GDR government and other state officials as well as academics and teachers has been more draconian than anything that was meted out to Nazi officials. It is as if the government is seeking exculpation for its antecedents not having dealt with the Nazi legacy appropriately and is therefore taking 'appropriate measures' this time round. Former Federal German Chancellor, Helmut Schmidt did, on several occasions, complain that after 1990 the communists were being more harshly treated than the Nazis had been.[81]

Thus the marginalisation and stigmatisation of a great number of intellectuals from the GDR was in stark contrast to what happened to former Nazis in the Federal Republic after the war. The 1951 amnesty law granted all those who had served under the Nazi regime the right of re-instatement in their previous jobs. This enabled 90 per cent of those

Nazi civil servants sacked in 1945 to return to public service.[82] It meant that professionals and academics who had not been merely apologists for fascism in Nazi Germany, but prominent ideologues, were able to return to their old positions without any real interruption and were even promoted to more influential positions in politics and state administration.

Nazi judges handed down around 60,000 death sentences on those opposed to the Hitler regime, but not one of these judges was brought to justice after the war. Hans Filbinger was a naval prosecutor under the Nazis and handed down a number of death sentences on those opposed to the Nazis. In the post-war era he rose to become First Minister of Baden-Wurttemberg and, with regard to those who accused him of being guilty of perverting the course of justice, he made the significant and notorious comment that 'What was right and just then, cannot be made unjust today'. This however clearly did not apply to the GDR, as the purges of East German intellectuals, described above, shows.

While the GDR had no statute of limitation on the prosecution of those who committed crimes against humanity, the Federal Republic did, although the law was amended in 1969 – extending the statute from 20 to 30 years – and again in 1979 to remove any limitation in cases of murder. Many of those who had been members of the Nazi elite or in the volunteer forces in the occupied territories were either not brought to justice or were amnestied and qualified for full German pension rights. Even members of the former Waffen-SS in Lithuania (some since living in the UK, USA or Australia) were granted war pensions. These were the same people who had helped the Nazis murder almost all the 70,000 Jews who lived in Lithuania before the war (and despite the fact that the Waffen-SS had been characterised as a criminal organisation by the Nuremberg War Crimes Tribunal).[83]

People from the GDR, however, were treated very differently. A special law was passed after unification which retrospectively provided legal justification for the reduction of pensions of those who worked in key positions for the GDR administration.[84]

It was those who had actually resisted and fought the Nazis who were invariably seen as traitors, underserving of recognition. This attitude was reflected in the banning by the West German government of the association of those persecuted by the Nazi regime (Die Vereinigung der Verfolgten des Naziregimes) which brought together and represented those who had suffered under the Hitler regime.

In the GDR, those who had actively resisted or suffered persecution by the Nazis had been granted an additional pension supplement; after unification, these pensions were reduced by 300 Deutsch Marks. Many who had resisted the Nazis and were forced to spend years in exile or were interned in prison or concentration camps found that those years were not pensionable under the West German pension system.

Former GDR citizens who were considered to be 'systemnah' (closely associated with the system) receive a reduced pension, often referred to as a 'punitive pension' (Strafrente). Following that pattern, a former lecturer at a GDR technical college was informed by the social security authorities that his GDR pension of 1,200 Deutsch Marks per month would be frozen while it was investigated whether this pension was an unlawful remuneration. He then informed the authorities that, as a young man, during the Hitler period, he had worked as a civil servant in Göring's air transport ministry. All of a sudden his pension was increased to an unbelievable 4,997 Deutsch Marks and on top of that he received a back payment of 149,000 Deutsch Marks. Working for the Nazi regime was of merit, but working for the GDR was reason for taking punitive measures.[85]

Even compensation offered to those considered to be victims of repression were dealt with using different criteria: those who were considered to have been wrongly imprisoned in the GDR received 550 Marks for each month spent in prison, whereas those who had been in Nazi concentration camps qualified for only 150 Deutsch Marks for each month of incarceration. This graphically illustrates the double standards used in the new unified Germany.[86]

All German military officers qualify for burial with full military honours, including those who served in Hitler's army, but not those who served in the GDR people's army. The message is: it was not ignoble to have served the Nazis but it was the communists.

There is little doubt that successive governments in West Germany after the war played down the role of the Nazis, simply by ignoring it. There were few if any films made or books published dealing with that legacy. For instance, Dachau, one of the few concentration camps to be located in the Western part of Germany was only established as a proper memorial as late as 1965. But immediately after unification, a whole number of museums were opened to show 'the horrors' of the GDR, like Hohenschönhausen the former Soviet and then GDR prison in Berlin.

When the GDR army was established in 1956, a number of those promoted to top positions in the armed services had acquired their military experience in the Spanish Civil War, fighting with the anti-fascists or, as prisoners during the Second World War, had rejected fascism and become active in the National Committee for a Free Germany. In contrast, in West Germany many former military officers who had served under the Nazis returned to their military careers. The former West German General, Gerd Bastian, told the author (JG) in a personal conversation that he joined the Bundeswehr after the war in the hope of helping to build a new democratic army but had been so shocked about the pervasive Nazi behaviour and ideology that he resigned and later became a leading member of the Green Party.

The German government evidently places more significance on dealing with the GDR than with the fascist period of German history. The Central Office in Ludwigsburg, Germany's main agency for the investigation of crimes committed by the Nazi regime had, at the height of its activity, five full-time employees. In comparison, the statutory authority examining the Stasi files has more than 3,000 employees and by 1998 had already cost the country around 1.39 billion Deutsch Marks.[87] And, significantly, despite a long and avid search by the present German authorities, tasked with analysing and taking out criminal proceedings against former Stasi officials for wrongdoing, only a tiny number have been convicted of any crime. Concrete evidence of serious mistreatment of individuals by the Stasi has been minimal.[88]

The tenacious vindictiveness and virulence with which the Federal German government has treated ex-GDR citizens and the whole historical legacy of the GDR, is an indication that anything connected with the idea of an alternative form of society is still seen as a threat.

The GDR not only carried out a thorough de-nazification but never ceased revealing how many old Nazis were back in power in the FRG and how reactionary its institutional structures still were and how the whole state was built on hypocritical foundations. In this sense the GDR held up a mirror reflecting an unflattering image of the West German state. When the opportunity arose (with the demise of the GDR and unification) to smash that mirror which had always reflected the ugly reality beneath the sheen of the West German 'economic wonder', it was grasped greedily with both hands. One could say, that all that damned up sense of guilt and shame was unleashed on the GDR and its citizens who became the scapegoat for all that was wrong in its own society. The GDR became the 'other totalitarian dictatorship', and its citizens – at least those who refused to accept this stigmatisation and their own 'guilt' of colluding with an 'illegal state' – were treated almost like outcasts but certainly like second class citizens.

CONCLUSION

The GDR was a small country of stark contradictions. It was an artificial state created on a third of the territory of the German nation. Two states grew up alongside each other, bound by family, cultural and national ties but divided by politics and ideology along Cold War lines.

It was a country that attempted to build socialism while facing a much larger and hostile capitalist nation on its western border and, at its back to the East, a dominating Soviet Union. It did not really conform to its self-declared description of a socialist workers' state, but nor was it a uniformly oppressive, totalitarian dictatorship.

Policy was firmly based on the long tradition of the progressive, humanistic and socialist strand in German history. Many people worked selflessly within that society for genuine humanitarian and democratic socialist goals and enjoyed considerable individual freedom and rewards. These aspects were also reflected in the GDR's literature and art, its theatres, popular song movement and rock scene, in the religious sphere and many other areas, where activities and culture gave expression to views very different from the official ones.

Many aspects of life in the GDR reflected genuine socialist elements while others were subject to authoritarian interference and a rigid paternalism. There were too many petty restrictions on people's freedoms on the one hand, but on the other, there was guaranteed social security, material support and social stability.

However, in the country and society as a whole, there was a disconnect between the humanistic goals to which both the leadership and most of the people aspired and the sometimes repressive manner of governing. A commando structure dominated and key decisions were taken with minimal involvement of the party's members or the wider population. Its leadership was divorced from the people's everyday concerns and had a paranoid fear of the enemy and about subversion. That is why it placed the state's security interests above a trust in its own people.[89]

There was little genuine debate or toleration of political dissent. And there was no real comprehension of the difference between 'public ownership' and 'state ownership' which was why a consciousness of public property as belonging to 'all of us' was not as highly developed as it should have been. Those contradictions, in the end, proved insurmountable and contributed considerably to the downfall of the GDR.

Recognition of these negative aspects, though, should not deflect from the genuine social progress that did take place. Despite everything, this small country made considerable advances and, above all, proved that a different society with different values is possible. Some of the most significant achievements include:

- the abolition of class privilege and the introduction of greater equality of income distribution
- elimination of land and property speculation
- restricting the influence of banks and other large financial institutions
- equal rights for women
- access to education for all
- promotion of the co-operative idea.

Since unification, and egged-on by the German establishment, the whole GDR experience has been predominantly interpreted by most Western writers and historians as one of 'totalitarianism' comparable with the

Nazi dictatorship; indeed the two systems are often bracketed together and condemned as the 'two totalitarian' periods of German history.

Over the two decades since the demise of the GDR, many of those who lived in the country have come to recognise and regret that the genuine social achievements they enjoyed have been dismantled. It is perhaps little wonder that many East Germans do not feel there has been a unification of two states, but that they have been taken over and treated as a colony of the West.

Western researchers have noted that in the recollections of those who lived in the GDR, the socialist state takes on a more positive aspect. This has been widely dismissed as 'Ostalgie' (a conflation of nostalgia and Osten [East]) – suggesting a rosy yearning for a mythical life in the GDR. However, those from East Germany have the advantage that they are able to compare both systems because they have experienced life in both. In retrospect, particular aspects of GDR society are seen as more significant today when compared to life in the West. For example, in a survey carried out in 1998, ex-GDR citizens were asked the question: 'From your own personal standpoint, to what extent do you associate life in the GDR with the following aspects?' The answers were very clear. On the positive side were full employment (89 per cent), social security (85 per cent), career opportunities for women (84 per cent), satisfaction in the workplace (65 per cent) and anti-fascism (54 per cent). Negative associations were restriction on travel (62 per cent), scarcity of consumer goods (42 per cent), domination of the SED (38 per cent), censorship (30 per cent) and being spied on (5 per cent).[90]

Mary Fulbrook observed in her book *The People's State*,[91] that 'Ostalgie' alone is not a sufficient explanation for the ways in which people did not recognise their own pasts in the new history textbooks outlining the structures of power and repression.' She says that history books that have focussed primarily on the institutions and practices of coercion are not necessarily wrong; but that they are to some degree incomplete, and are predicated on an over-simplistic model of the ways in which the GDR system worked, and the ways in which it changed over time. This is corroborated by first-hand accounts given by former GDR citizens themselves.

The more positive attitudes to their state held by many ex-GDR citizens has been underlined in a series of post-unification surveys and studies carried out by respected organisations and research institutes. In a report on a survey of East Germans made in 1997, Professor Noelle-Neumann from the Allensbach Institute for Demoscopy wrote: 'Two thirds think that in essence it was a good time, and that the principles on which the GDR was based were also good'.[92]

And in 2009, according to a survey by the Emnid Institute, more than half of East Germans saw the GDR 'in a positive light, that it had more good than bad sides and one could live well'. In contrast, 78 per cent of West Germans saw the GDR as 'overwhelmingly bad'.[93] On the basis of this survey, Wolfgang Tiefensee, the Federal Government Commissioner for the East, said 'more educational work was needed to explain inter-German history' in order to redress this mistaken perception.[94] This view was reiterated by the Berlin sociologist Klaus Schroeder (Director of the research association for the study of the SED state), who was outraged that many East Germans still, in 2008, saw any criticism of the system in the GDR as an attack on themselves and rejected the labeling of their country as an 'Unrechtsstaat.'[95]

All these surveys underline the fact that in people's experience and their memories of life in the GDR there was much that was positive, and compared with their experience of capitalism, that life did offer stability, full employment and a sense of social purpose and common culture. Even today, 25 years after unification, many Germans refer to 'Ossies' and 'Wessies' in tacit recognition of the persistent cultural differences that still exist.

To illustrate, here are some excerpts from interviews made with several ex-GDR citizens from a variety of backgrounds. They have the benefit of being able to compare their present lives in a unified, capitalist Germany with those they led in the GDR.[96]

Karin an architect: 'After unification, I noticed that western architects think in a completely different way. As architects we are socially responsible to society for the built-up environment. I think architects should swear a sort of Hippocratic oath to work for the wellbeing of mankind just as doctors do.' Despite the oft condescending comments about 'socialist barrack-block buildings', GDR architects were often able to plan and build in an integrated and co-ordinated way; they wouldn't just design a shop or an old people's home in isolation, but would look at the whole area and could design buildings that were integrated better into the fabric of the locality. Because of the largely private land ownership in the West such architectural planning is rarely possible. 'Only after unification did I realise, what level of gender equality we had in the GDR. We also experienced a carefree, protected childhood. Then we had the communities formed in the workplace, in the holiday centres, a good school and committed teachers. I experienced all that consciously and so I know what it feels like to live without the continuous threat to one's existence ...'

The car mechanic Michael had been a spokesperson for a Catholic student group in his youth and certainly no apologist for the GDR. He had experienced no problems studying and obtaining the qualifications he needed and went on to open up his own car repair shop. He relates: 'In the pioneer centres you could build models, do motor sport, various crafts or sing; now young people do little else but go to the disco. What I particularly miss today is the comradeship and friendships I had in GDR times. I find it difficult to adapt to this elbow society.'

The farm worker Christa Erdmann: 'In the village we supported each other. In the evening after work my brothers came, sometimes a neighbour and helped with the building [of our new house]. That was very different from now. There wasn't the envy there is today. Now they put it in your employment contract that if you tell anybody what you earn, it's a sacking offence. In GDR times everyone knew what everyone else earned. What's bad about that? That's how mistrust arises and even suspicion is enough to create divisions among people.'

The GP Regina: 'Material wealth was no big issue for me … we didn't study medicine to earn heaps of money. During our studies and in our work a humanistic ideal was imbued in us, and we carried out our work with that ethos. If I had a wish today, I'd just like to be an ordinary doctor once again. Free from all the budgeting and free from all these accounting constraints.' In an interview with the author (BdM) in 1990, another working doctor characterised the change in attitudes to the health service since unification thus: it is a change from 'a medical ethos to a monetary ethos'.

The socialist experience did offer a different narrative. Most individuals within society felt they had more control over their own destinies because of a guaranteed social stability: the GDR did not go through comparable economic crises, but demonstrated a continuing rise in living standards and individual wellbeing. What needs to be learned is how it was possible that the dreams and aspirations of so many good and well-intentioned individuals could be distorted and undermined.

Both before and since the demise of the GDR, western leaders and pundits have continuously devalued anything and everything that was undertaken during the years of communist-led government. There has been little interest or desire by progressives and those on the left to undertake a serious debate or evaluation of this attempt to build a socialist society. No genuine attempt has been made to assess what really went wrong and why, nor if anything could be considered worth emulating. We have had only a blanket condemnation of totalitarianism. We have been continually inoculated against the contagious virus of socialism by stock images of a Stasi-run, tyrannical and soulless state, grey, faceless housing blocks, shops devoid of goods and an oppressed people – a depressing uniformity everywhere.

Significantly, the GDR, just like Cuba or Venezuela today, has rarely been criticised or attacked for having failed to create a genuine socialist democracy but rather for 'having the effrontery' of attempting to do so in the first place. Socialism is, in many quarters, still seen as an alien ideology. This attitude was reflected in Chancellor Helmut Kohl's 1976 election slogan: 'Freedom instead of socialism, for love of Germany' – and that was aimed at the SPD! This slogan with a slight difference – 'Socialism or Freedom' was resuscitated by the CDU during the first election in the re-united Germany. Socialism is portrayed as inimical to freedom and democracy.

A denigration of socialism is in the vested interest of capitalism, particularly because the concept could still be useful in suggesting answers to a crisis-ridden and unjust capitalism. We can learn from this short-lived attempt at building such a society, even though it took place in a Cold War context, under adverse circumstances not of its people's own choosing.

One important impact made by the GDR and the socialist world is often overlooked, and that is the positive effect they had on social policies in the West. During the life of the GDR, it was often noted by trade unionists in West Germany that when negotiating with employers the

GDR was invariably an important but invisible presence at the negotiating table, i.e. there was always an awareness on both sides of what was happening in the GDR in terms of workers' rights.

There is little doubt that the establishment of the welfare state in most western European countries was largely in response to the impact of the Bolshevik Revolution. The ruling establishments feared socialist revolutions in their own countries and realised that only by offering working people an amelioration of their conditions and granting increased rights in the workplace would they be able to head off more revolutionary demands. This was reinforced after the defeat of fascism in 1945 in alliance with the Soviet Union and the widespread desire for more radical social policies in the post-war world.

While the East European socialist bloc had indeed a democratic deficit in terms of political rights, its economic and welfare rights were valued and represented an incentive for change even in the West. Certainly in the Federal Republic of Germany, much of its quite generous post-war welfare policies, trade union rights and social insurance provision were developed in direct response to what the GDR had introduced, and with the aim of countering any potential attractiveness of socialist policies.

It is no coincidence that the large-scale attacks on the welfare state in the West have coincided with the demise of the socialist world. Now there is no concrete alternative on offer, the capitalist world has taken the gloves off.

It is quite amazing and also alarming how easily one narrative, given sufficient media coverage and promotion, is able to marginalise all others, and how willing so many are to accept this as the whole truth without making the effort to delve deeper or question widely held assumptions. That has been the case with the GDR.

What the GDR did achieve is the encouragement and development of a social conscience among the people, the idea of placing the good of society at the centre of social activities, not individualism, as well as the elaboration of clear social goals to which the majority can subscribe.

Those 40 years in which the GDR survived represent a genuine attempt to build a socialist society and its experience offers us all lessons and insights if we are willing to look for them. It contained a whole number of elements and experiences that could and should inform any future attempts to build a socialist society and help avoid such deformations that were so fatal for previous ones and which provided such invaluable ammunition for the real enemies of socialism.

So how can we draw up a balance sheet for the GDR? What sort of society was it? The title of our book provocatively suggests it was either of two extremes, but in reality it was neither. It was not a 'totalitarian' or 'unjust' state in the mould of the Hitler regime or other repressive dictatorships, but nor was it a paragon of socialist democracy and justice. It was a state of contradictions. Society was organised on a socially just basis. People were guaranteed stability, a secure job and housing, access to healthcare, culture and education. Individuals felt that they were socially useful and valued and this gave many people a satisfying justification for their lives. But political structures were rigid, there was top-down, hierarchical decision-making and an often claustrophobic patronising attitude; there was a paranoid fear of opposition and subversion which soured relationships between the people and the ruling party. The GDR was a socialist state with serious and, in the end, terminally fatal defects. We can learn both from what it achieved in terms of an attempt to create a more just society, as well as from what went wrong and why it failed.

NOTES

1   Horst Schneider, "Die Volkskongressbewegung fuer Einheit und gerechten Frieden", in: Gerhard Fischer, Hans-Joachim Krusch, Hans Modrow, Wolfgang Richter, Robert Steigerwald, eds. *Gegen den Zeitgeist. Zwei deutsche Staaten in der Geschichte* (Schkeuditz: GNN Verlag,1999), pp.52-57.

2   Siegfried Wenzel, *Die DDR-Wirtschaft im Spannungsfeld zwischen objektiven Bedingungen und Politik der SED*, in: Ludwig Elm, Dietmar Keller, Reinhard Mocek, eds. *Ansichten zur Geschichte der DDR, Band VI*, (Eggersdorf: Verlag Matthias Kirchner, 1996), p.97.

3   Otto Köhler. *Die Grosse Enteignung – wie die Treuhand eine Volkswirtschaft liquidierte*, (Berlin: Verlag Das Neue Berlin, 2011)

4   16 per cent of members of the first post-war SED politbureau were from a Jewish background.

5   Jutta Ditfurth, *Durch Unischtbare Mauern; wie wird eine links?*, (Köln: Kiepenheuer & Witsch, 2002) p.100

6   In the Western zones 5,025 Nazis were convicted, 806 of those were given a death sentence, but only 486 were carried out.

7   Thomas Mann, *Tagebücher 28.5.1946-31.12.1948* (Frankfurt-am-Main: S. Fischer Verlag, 1989) p.233

8   Ekkehard Lieberam, "Der Sozialstaatskompromiss und dessen Erosion", in: Gerhard Fischer, Hans-Joachim Krusch, Hans Modrow, Wolfgang Richter, Robert Steigerwald, eds. *Gegen den Zeitgeist. Zwei deutsche Staaten in der Geschichte* (Schkeuditz: GNN Verlag,1999), p.164.

9   Jutta Ditfurth, *Durch Unischtbare Mauern; wie wird eine links?*, p.15.

10   Jonathan Steele, *Socialism with a German Face*, (London: Jonathan Cape, 1977)

11   In 1964, an East German freighter, the MV Magdeburg, with 42 Leyland buses bound for Cuba, made its way down the Thames. It was rammed and sunk by a Japanese ship. This was in all likelihood a CIA-directed operation targeting both the GDR and Cuba. See Tracy McVeigh and Andrew Rosthorn, *The Observer,* Sunday 26 October 2008.

12 *Der Spiegel* 24 Feb 1965

13 In October 1945 both the Communist Party and the Social
    Democratic Party in the East opened a joint campaign calling for the
    banning of war toys. The West German Bundestag also passed a law
    banning the production and sale of military toys in June 1950, but it
    was easily circumvented and was more a statement of intention than
    practice. With the establishment of new military blocs (NATO in
    1949 and the Warsaw Pact in 1955) and the re-establishment of
    German armies, first in the West (1955) and then in the East (1956),
    military toys were again legitimised. Although there were widespread
    protests in the East against this re-introduction, including by a
    number of church leaders.

14 It should be emphasised, though, that the separation of Party and
    state leadership from the mass of the people was not based on
    economic privilege. Despite some post-unification lurid and
    apocryphal tales about Erich Honecker's purported Swiss bank
    account and the luxurious living standards enjoyed by leading
    figures, reality was in fact more mundane. While they did enjoy
    privileges not enjoyed by ordinary working people, these were still
    extremely modest by Western standards. No one owned luxury
    mansions or had foreign bank accounts nor did they amass great
    personal wealth; with the demise of the GDR, they all became
    dependent on their state pensions for survival. Nor was the GDR's
    leadership characterised by endemic corruption.

15 Wolfgang Engler, *Die Ostdeutschen* (Berlin: Aufbau Verlag, 1999)

16 Stefan Bollinger/Fritz Vilmar. eds. *Die DDR war anders. Eine kritische
    Würdigung ihrer sozialkulturellen Einrichtungen.* (Berlin: edition ost, 2002)

17 Claudia Wangerin, *Die DDR und ihre Töchter.* (Berlin: Verlag Das
    Neue Berlin, 2010). On the wages front, the wage differential
    between men and women in the GDR was around 5 per cent, but in
    the West it was 25 per cent. The German Government Office for
    Statistics bears this out when, in November 2009, it noted that
    women from the East are more often in possession of technical
    qualifications through their careers and that such jobs are better paid
    than 'typically female' ones. (Wangerin, p.171)

18 *Der Spiegel* "20 Jahre DDR" No 41/1969

19 Wolfgang Plat. in *Der Spiegel* No. 38/1971

20 Bernd Schepeler. *Wie konnte das geschehen?* (Norderstedt: Verlag BoD,
    2014), pp.55f.

21 Schepeler

22 Peter Hübner. *Konsens, Konflikt und Kompromiss. Soziale Arbeiterinteressen*

und Sozialpolitik der SBZ/DDR 1945-1970 (Berlin: Akademie Verlag, 1995)

23 Mary Fulbrook, *The People's State – East German Society from Hitler to Honecker* (New Haven and London: Yale University Press, 2005)

24 Jutta Ditfurth, *Durch Unsichtbare Mauern; wie wird eine links?*, p.60.

25 Fulbrook, p.286.

26 Fulbrook, p.78.

27 Daniela Dahn, *Westwärts und nicht Vergessen* (Berlin: Rowohlt, 1996), pp.184f.

28 Peter Grabley, 'Das eigentliche Wirtschaftswunder', in: Katrin Rohnstock (ed.), *Jetzt Reden Wir*, p.57.

29 Köhler

30 Wolfgang Richter, 'Reprivatisierung im Osten', Gegen den Zeitgeist, p.369
In 1987, the UN published a development programme in which it listed the per capita GDP of the world's leading 130 states. According to this, 110 of those states had a lower GDP than the GDR.

31 Olaf Baale, *Abbau Ost. Lügen, Vorurteile und sozialistische Schulden* (München: Deutscher Taschenbuch Verlag, 2008)

32 *Die Kombinatsdirektoren. Jetzt reden wir.* (Berlin: edition berolina, 2014) p.65

33 Wenzel, p.89.

34 Gerhard Schürer. *Gewagt und verloren. Eine deutsche Biographie.* (Berlin: edition ost, 2014 [1998])

35 Heiner Rubarth, 'Innovation und Improvisation in der DDR-Industrie', in: Katrin Rohnstock (ed.), *Die Kombinationsdirektoren*, p.91.

36 Hannah Behrend (ed.) *The German Unification. The Destruction of an Economy* (London: Pluto Press, 1995), p.181.

37 Hans Luft, "Von der LPG zur Agrargenossenschaft: eine positive Entwicklung?", in: Stefan Bollinger/Fritz Vilmar (eds.), *Die DDR war anders. Eine kritische Würdigung ihrer sozialkulturellen Einrichtungen.* (Berlin: edition ost, 2009), p.214.

38 Luft, p.216.

39 Gerd Dietrich. "Kulturgeschichte der DDR – wie angehen und darstellen?", in: *Kulturation Online*. Journal für Kultur, Wissenschaft und Politik No. 18/2015

40 Fulbrook

41 Frances Stonor Saunders. *The Cultural Cold War: The CIA and the World of Arts and Letters.* (New York: The New Press, 2000)

42   Panorama DDR (ed.) *Fragen und Antworten – Leben in der DDR*
     (Berlin: Verlag Zeit im Bild, 1981)

43   David Childs. *East Germany* (London: Ernest Benn, 1969)

44   Stefan Volk. "Banned Films in the Federal Republic – the censor and
     the Cold War", *Spiegel Magazine* Online, 7 July 2014

45   Franziska Kleiner. *Was von der DDR blieb* (Berlin: Eulenspiegel Verlag,
     2009), pp.185ff.

46   Paul Ginsborg, *Democracy – Crisis and Renewal* (London: Profile
     Books, 2008), p.79.

47   Dahn, *Westwärts und nicht Vergessen*, p.121.

48   Dahn, *Westwärts und nicht Vergessen*, p.123.

49   Oda Lambrecht, Christian Decker, 'Verurteilte Schwuhle: 'Eine
     Schande bis heute'. *NDR.de. Panorama*. 7.4.2015.

50   Peter Maxwill, "25 Jahre Deutsche Einheit: Kinder, Autos, Religion -
     der Ost-West-Vergleich"
     Spiegel online politik, 22.07.2015;

51   German Bundestag Enquete-Kommission. Aufarbeitung von
     Geschichte und Folgen der SED-Diktatur in Deutschland,
     Drucksache 12/7820, p.229.

52   Ralph Hartmann. *Die DDR unterm Lügenberg* (Berlin: edition ost,
     2010)

53   Daniela Dahn "Der Waschzwang des Staates – Wem gehört die
     Gauck-Behörde?" Süddeutsche Zeitung 17./18.1.1998.

54   Hans Modrow, *Perestroika and Germany – the truth behind the myths*
     (London: Marx Memorial Library and Artery Publications, 2014)

55   Willy Brandt was also opposed to the unification of the two
     German states but was in favour of a confederation, however, by
     1990 he also realised that "the ship had already sailed; unification is
     the only option.'" quoted in: Jürgen Kuczynski, *Freunde und Gute
     Bekannte*, Schwarzkopf & Schwarzkopf, 1997, p.147.

56   Hans Modrow, *Perestroika and Germany – the truth behind the myths*

57   Schepeler, p.186.

58   Schepeler, pp.185f.

59   TASS correspondent's report, 19 March 1990, quoted by Hartmann,
     Liquidatoren, p.36.

60   When Saarland joined Germany in 1956 – pre-war it belonged to
     France – it was granted a transition period of several years during
     which its products and markets enjoyed special protection, and this
     despite the fact that, unlike the GDR, it had a similar economic
     system.

61   Baale, p.63.

62 Klaus Huhn, *Raubzug Ost. Wie die Treuhand die DDR plünderte* (Berlin: edition ost, 2009), p.17.

63 Huhn, p.17.

64 Köhler, p.93.

65 Köhler, pp.96f.

66 Schepeler, p.186.

67 Reiner Maria Gohlke, former top manager of IBM and then Chief Executive of German Railways, was brought out of retirement by Chancellor Kohl to take over the presidency of the national trusteeship quango (Treuhand) immediately after the GDR elections in March 1990. He stated in August 1990: 'I had absolutely no doubt that the renovation of the GDR economy was one of the great challenges of our time. I remained optimistic that the economy on the basis of its resources, particularly the ready availability of engineers and technical expertise, represented a great opportunity; I was not of the opinion that there was little enthusiasm on the part of national or international interests to invest or participate in this process.' Gohlke only remained in the job a few weeks, to be replaced by a more hard line privateer.

68 In 1987, the UNO issued a development programme in which it listed 130 states according to their gross domestic products per head of the population. 110 of these states had a lower GDP than the GDR, among them EU states like Portugal and Greece as well as all Comecon states. Gerhard Fischer et al., p.369.

69 State farms were big ones where sector-specific research and development took place.

70 Huhn, p.22.

71 Huhn, p.23.

72 Gerhard Beil, *Aussenhandel und Politik – ein Minister erinnert sich* (Berlin: edition ost, 2010), p.276.

73 Dieter Kampe, *Wer uns kennenlernt gewinnt uns lieb. Nachruf auf die Treuhand* (Berlin: Rotbuch Verlag, 1993)

74 Robert Ide, *Geteilte Träume. Meine Eltern, die Wende und ich*, (München: Luchterhand, 2007)

75 Wirtschaftskriminalität im Einigungsprozess aus Politik und Zeitgeschichte (B 32-33/2001) Bundesdeutsche Zentrale für politische Bildung (26 May 2002)

76 Baale, p.27.

77 Karl Albrecht Schachtschneider. *Sozialistische Schulden nach der Revolution. Kritik der Altschuldenpolitik. Ein Beitrag zur Lehre von Recht und Unrecht* (Berlin: Verlagsbuchhandlung Duncker & Humblot, 1996)

78   Dahn, *Wehe dem Sieger*, p.153.
79   With the 'Radikalenerlass' of 1972 in the Federal Republic, 3.5 million political checks were carried out on those applying for posts in the public services; in 35,000 cases incriminating evidence was forwarded to prospective employers – alongside sackings and disciplinaries – around 10,000 individuals were blacklisted. Jutta Ditfurth, *Durch Unischtbare Mauern; wie wird eine links?*, (Kiepenheuer & Witsch, 2002) p.280
80   Schepeler, p.126.
81   Dahn, *Wehe dem Sieger*, p.99.
82   Müller, Ingo, *Furchtbare Juristen. Die unbewältigte Vergangenheit unserer Justiz.* (München: Kindler, 1987)
83   Daniela Dahn, "Die Braunlage", Kursbuch, No.162 (2005)
84   According to a law introduced by the German government immediately after unification, whole groups of former GDR citizens were to be subjected to reduced pension rights. It stipulates, that the following former GDR citizens were to receive significantly reduced pensions for the period in which they were employed by the state, amongst them secretaries of state, ministers, secretaries and their deputies in national and regional government; departmental heads of the central committee of the SED and all staff of the security services; the state prosecutor in the State Attorney's Office of the GDR and members of the regional or district operation control.
85   Daniela Dahn, *Wehe dem Siege*,. p.99.
86   Daniela Dahn. *Westwärts und nicht Vergessen*, p.45.
87   Daniela Dahn "Der Waschgang des Staates – Wem gehört die Gauck Behörde?", in: Daniela Dahn, *Vertreibung ins Paradies* (Berlin: Rowohlt, 1998)
88   Since unification, over 75,000 investigations were undertaken by the German Public Prosecutor against 100,000 suspects but the number of suspects fell dramatically during the investigative process. In the end, only 1.4 per cent of those under investigation were actually put on trial (1,021). Most of those found guilty of a crime were given fines. Klaus Marxen, Gerhard Werle, Petra Schäfter. *Die Strafregelung von DDR-Unrecht Fakten und Zahlen* (Berlin: Stiftung der Aufarbeitung der SED-Diktatur Humboldt University, 2007)
89   SFZ-Beiträge zur sozialen Transformation, Band 13, Berlin 1998. (SFZ – Sozialwissenschaftliches Forschungszentrum)
90   Fulbrook, pp.3f.

91 *Frankfurter Allgemeine Zeitung*, 10 December1997.
92 "Studie: Ostdeutsche sehen DDR positive", *Merkur Online* 26 June 2009.
93 *Focus Online* 26 June2009
94 "Mit dem Mauerfall aus dem Paradies vertrieben", *Spiegel Online*, 28 June 2009
95 Erika Maier. *Einfach leben - hüben wie drüben* (Berlin: Karl Dietz Verlag, 2007. The journalist Erika Maier, who grew up in the GDR, wrote this book, she says, because she got so tired of hearing the refrain: 'How could you East Germans stand it – this GDR state, the paternalism, locked in, spied on by the Stasi?' She realised that those who had never lived in the GDR could never understand fully what daily life was like. Therefore she decided to interview 12 'pairs' of individuals with comparable jobs, one from the East and their counterpart from the West. These biographies illustrate how different the experiences and values in East and West were.

BIBLIOGRAPHY

Andert, Reinhold. *Nach dem Sturz - Gespräche mit Erich Honecker* (Leipzig: Faber & Faber, 2001)

Arp, Agnes and Annette Leo. *Mein Land verschwand so schnell… 16 Lebensgeschichten und die Wende 1989/90.* (Weimar: wtv-campus Verlag, 2009)

Bisky, Lothar u.a. (eds.) *Die PDS – Herkunft und Selbstverständnis* (Berlin: Dietz Verlag, 1996)

Baale, Olaf. *Abbau Ost. Lügen, Vorurteile und sozialistische Schulden* (Muenchen: Deutscher Taschenbuch Verlag, 2008)

Becker, Johannes M. *Ein Land geht in den Westen: die Abwicklung der DDR* (Bonn: Dietz Taschenbuch, 1991)

Behrend, Hanna (ed.): *The German Unification. The Destruction of an Economy* (London: Pluto Press, 1995)

Beil, Gerhard. *Aussenhandel und Politik. Ein Minister erinnert sich* (Berlin: edition ost, 2010)

Brombacher, Ellen, Thomas Hecker, Juergen Herold, Friedrich Rabe and Werner Wueste (eds.) *Klartexte – Beitraege zur Gechichtsdebatte* (Berlin: verlag am park, 2009)

Bollinger, Stefan and Fritz Vilmar (eds.) *Die DDR war anders. Eine kritische Wuerdigung ihrer sozialkulturellen Einrichtungen* (Berlin: edition ost, 2002)

Childs, David. *East Germany* (London: Ernest Benn, 1969)

Dahn, Daniela. *Wir bleiben hier oder Wem gehoert der Osten* (Reinbeck: Rowohlt, 1994)

Dahn, Daniela. *Westwaerts und nicht vergessen. Vom Unbehagen in der Einheit* (Berlin: Rowohlt, 1996)

Dahn, Daniela. *Vertreibung ins Paradies* (Reinbeck: Rowohlt, 1998)

Dahn, Daniela. *Wenn und Aber* (Reinbeck: Rowohlt, 2002)

Dahn, Daniela. „Die Braunlage", Kursbuch, No. 162 (2005)

Dahn, Daniela. *Wehe dem Sieger! Ohne Osten kein Westen* (Reinbeck: Rowohlt, 2009)

Dahlke, Ernst, Holger Becker and Bernd Bludau. Abwicklung von Einrichtungen der Wissenschaft und des Hochschulwesens der ehemaligen DDR. Eine Dokumentation. (Berlin, 1991)

Dennis, Mike. *German Democratic Republic – Politics, Economics and Society*

(London and New York: Pinter Publishers, 1988)

Dümcke, Wolfgang und Vilmar, Fritz (eds.); *Kolonisierung der DDR: Kritische Analysen und Alternativen des Einigungsprozesses* (Muenster:agenda Verlag, 1995)

Elm, Ludwig, Dietmar Keller, Reinhard Mocek (eds.) *Ansichten zur Geschichte der DDR, Band VI,* (Eggersdorf: Verlag Matthias Kirchner, 1996)

Engler, Wolfgang. *Die Ostdeutschen – Kunde von einem verlorenen Land* (Berlin: Aufbau Verlag, 1999)

Fischer, Gerhard, Hans-Joachim Krusch, Hans Modrow, Wolfgang Richter, Robert Steigerwald (eds.) *Gegen den Zeitgeist. Zwei deutsche Staaten in der Geschichte* (Schkeuditz: GNN Verlag,1999)

Fulbrook, Mary. *The People's State* (New Haven/London: Yale University Press, 2008)

Ginsborg, Paul. *Democracy – Crisis and renewal* (London: Profile Books, 2008)

Grass, Günther. *Ein Schnäppchen namens DDR* (Frankfurt am Main: Luchterhand, 1990)

Grossman, Victor. *Crossing the River: A Memoir of the American Left, the Cold War and Life in East Germany* (Boston: University of Massachusetts Press, 2003)

Gysi, Gregor. *Das war's. Noch lange nicht!* (München: Econ & List Taschenbuch Verlag, 1999)

Hartmann, Ralph. *Die Liquidatoren: der Reichskommissar und das wiedergewonnene Vaterland* (Berlin: Verlag Neues Leben, 1996)

Hartmann, Ralph. *Die DDR unterm Lügenberg* (Berlin: edition ost, 2010)

Hensel, Jana. *Zonenkinder* (Berlin: Rowohlt, 2003)

Herlt, Günter. *Birne contra Historie* (Berlin: Spotless Verlag, no date)

Herlt, Günter. *Sendeschluss* (Berlin: Edition Ost, 1995)

Herzog, Lothar. *Honecker Privat – Ein Personenschützer Berichtet* (Berlin: edition berolina, 2013)

Holm, Knut. *Das Charité Komplott* (Berlin: Spotless Verlag, 1991)

Huhn, Klaus. *Raubzug Ost: Wie die Treuhand die DDR plünderte* (Berlin: edition ost, 2009)

Hübner, Peter. *Konsens, Konflikt und Kompromiss. Soziale Arbeiterinteressen und Sozialpolitik der SBZ/DDR 1945-1970* (Berlin: Akademie Verlag, 1995)

Jackson, Paul (ed.) *DDR- Das Ende eines Staates* (Manchester University Press, 1994)

Jung, H. et al (eds). *BRD-DDR. Vergleich der Gesellschaftssysteme* (Koeln: Pahl Rugenstein Verlag, 1971)

Kleiner, Franziska. *Was von der DDR blieb* (Berlin: Eulenspiegel Verlag, 2009)

Kampe, Dieter. *Wer uns kennenlernt gewinnt uns lieb. Nachruf auf die Treuhand* (Berlin: Rotbuch Verlag, 1993)

Köhler, Otto. *Die Grosse Enteignung. Wie die Treuhand eine Volkswirtschaft liquidierte.* (Berlin: Verlag Das Neue Berlin, 2011)

Kotz, David and Fred Weir. *Revolution from Above – the Demise of the Soviet System* (London: Routledge, 1997)

Kuczynski, Juergen, *Memoiren* (4 volumes) (Berlin: Aufbau Verlag, 1981; 1994; 1998; 1999)

Liedtke, Ruediger (ed.) *Die Treuhand und die zweite Enteignung der Ostdeutschen* (Muenchen: edition spangenberg, 1993)

Lindner, Gabriele *Die Eigenart der Implosion. Lange Genese bis zu Modrow-Regierung und Rundem Tisch in der DDR* (Berlin: Kolog Verlag, 1994)

Luft, Christa. *Die nächste Wende kommt bestimmt* (Berlin: Aufbau Taschenbuch Verlag, 1994)

Maier Erika. *Einfach leben – hueben wie drueben.* Zwoelf Doppelbiographien (Berlin: Karl Dietz Verlag, 2007)

Meer, Horst van der and Lothar Kruss (eds) *Von Industriestaat zum Entwicklungsland?* (Frankfurt/Main: Joester Vertriebsgemeinschaft, 1991)

Modrow, Hans. *Perestroika and Germany. The Truth Behind the Myths* (London: Marx Memorial Library and Artery Publications, 2014)

Modrow, Hans. *Aufbruch und Ende* (Berlin: edition berolina, 2013)

Müller, Ingo. *Furchtbare Juristen – die unbewältigte Vergangenheit unserer Justiz* (München: Kindler, 1987)

Mueller, Heiner. *Zur Lage der Nation* (Berlin: Rotbuch Verlag, 1990)

Panorama DDR (ed.) *Fragen und Antworten – Leben in der DDR* (Berlin: Verlag Zeit im Bild, 1981)

Radice, Giles. *The New Germans* (London: Michael Joseph, 1995)

Rohnstock, Katrin (ed.) *Stiefschwestern. Was Ost-Frauen und West-Frauen voneinander denken* (Frankfurt/Main: Fischer Taschenbuch Verlag, 1994)

Rohnstock biografien (ed.) *Jetzt Reden Wir – Was heute aus der DDR-Wirtschaft zu lernen ist* (Berlin: edition berolina, 2014)

Schachtschneider, Karl Albrecht. *Sozialistische Schulden nach der Revolution. Kritik der Altschuldenpolitik. Ein Beitrag zur Lehre von Recht und Unrecht* (Berlin: Verlagsbuchhandlung Duncker & Humblot, 1996)

Schepeler, Bernd. *Wie konnte das geschehen? Ansichten ueber das Scheitern der DDR* (Norderstedt: Verlag BoD, 2014)

Schnitzler, Karl-Eduard von. *Der Rote Kanal. Armes Deutschland* (Hamburg: Nautilus, 1992)

Schürer, Gerhard. *Gewagt und verloren. Eine deutsche Biographie.* (Berlin: edition ost, 1998)

Simmons, Michael, *The Unloved Country – a portrait of East Germany Today* (London: Abacus, 2014 [1998])

Steele, Jonathan. *Socialism with a German Face. The state that came in from the cold* (London: Jonathan Cape, 1977)

Stonor Saunders, Frances, *The Cultural Cold War: The CIA and the World of Arts and Letters.* (New York: The New Press, 2000)

Szepansky, Gerda. *Die Stille Emanzipation: Frauen in der DDR* (Frankfurt/Main: Fischer Taschenbuch Verlag, 1995)

Shaw, Elizabeth. *Wie ich nach Berlin kam. Eine Irin in der geteilten Stadt* (Berlin: Verlag fuer Berlin-Brandenburg, 2013)

Voigt, Jutta. *Im Osten geht die Sonne auf – Berichte aus anderen Zeiten* (Berlin-Brandenburg: be.bra verlag, 2009)

Wangerin, Claudia. *Die DDR und ihre Toechter* (Berlin: Verlag Das Neue Berlin, 2010)